HAUNTED FERRY PLANTATION

HAUNTED FERRY PLANTATION

KRISTEN P. ELLIS

Haunted America

Published by Haunted America
A division of The History Press
An imprint of Arcadia Publishing
Charleston, SC
www.historypress.com

First published 2025

Manufactured in the United States

ISBN 9781467157759

Library of Congress Control Number: 2025937580

This book is dedicated to my parents, Bill and Sue Mitchell, who instilled in me a love of history; to my brother, Scott, who showed me how to make history come alive by sharing it with others; and to the incredible volunteers of Ferry Plantation, who have become like family through our shared love and passion for this amazing place we all call home.

CONTENTS

FOREWORD

Growing up in Virginia Beach, I heard a lot of stories about the "Witch's House." This was years before Louisa Venable Kyle's book *The Witch of Pungo* was released in 1974. In a way, that book supported the stories. There was a witch, but not in Pungo. And although she never lived in the house, she was supposedly confined there for her "trial by water" in the nearby Lynnhaven River. Historically, an accused witch was ducked into a body of water several times (hence Witchduck Road). The idea was that the water was pure and would reject anything evil. Death by drowning meant innocence, but the accused's soul was with God. Surviving meant that the defendant was indeed a witch and would put to death by hanging or burning at the stake.

All this intrigued me, and I decided I had to see this house myself. It was just a short trip from where I lived, less than ten miles. Compared to now, the two main boulevards leading to the house were narrow roadways. With no GPS or signage to guide me, I did make a did make a few U-turns before I anxiously reached my destination. As I made one final turn, I saw the big house looming ahead. For a brief moment, I thought I had arrived at 1313 Mockingbird Lane (home of the Munsters, for those of you who are not fans of classic TV).

The surrounding thirty acres of land bore evidence of a young, growing neighborhood, but at this time there were no homes within two hundred yards of the Witch's House. It stood alone. Around the property there was a tall chain link fence. On the gate was a padlock and a bright-red sign with

"No Trespassing" in white letters. There were a few old trees, and what grass there was reached about two feet high. There was a mix of weeds and debris, mostly downed branches and broken pieces of the house.

The house itself was ominous—long abandoned, neglected, doors boarded up and windows framed in shards of glass. The eaves, the porch and the stairs were obviously decayed. It certainly made all the ghost stories believable, and I would swear I saw a pale, emaciated face looking down at me from one of the windows.

So much has happened since those days. I was a regular presence there for several years. I was there for kids' summer camps, sometimes as a Civil War soldier and sometimes as a pirate. My Haunted Investigation Team (HIT) spent several nights there and experienced several unexplainable things, both audible and visible. Ghost hunters from all over the state pay to investigate and try to contact any of the fourteen spirits believed to be in the house.

But it's not just a haunted house. It is now a popular stop for visitors wishing to see all of Virginia Beach's historic houses. It is host to several educational programs like "high tea" served in the dining room, as well as other events.

As a historian and the president of the Princess Anne County/Virginia Beach Historical Society, I appreciate the house's valuable place in our local history, dating back to the seventeenth century. It burned down in the eighteenth century. It was rebuilt in the nineteenth century. It was abandoned and rebuilt again in the twentieth century.

Kristen Ellis has extensively researched the facts and the legends of this place and time and has organized this information into several unique chapters. Each one tells an individual story, and when joined together, they provide an informative description of the Ferry House and its related history.

—ALPHEUS CHEWNING
Author of *Haunted Virginia Beach*,
Virginia Beach in Vintage Postcards and *Virginia Shipwrecks*

Preface

On my endless quest of visiting haunted locations, I first came to Ferry Plantation House in July 2019. The volunteers were hosting a Friday Night Frights, where guests can explore the house with a guide, learning about the history, the hauntings and evidence gathered from paranormal investigations. As I turned off the main road, the GPS said I was getting close, but I was engulfed by a neighborhood of large luxury homes, perched along the banks of the Lynnhaven River. I was sure I was lost, as this certainly couldn't be the location of a nineteenth-century historic home. But as I rounded a bend in the road, I saw the sign and then caught a glimpse of the old house tucked back at the end of a long brick sidewalk. As I walked up to the home, I noticed how out of place it looked in the middle of this modern neighborhood. However, the closer I got, I saw its strength, its perseverance and its wisdom as it stood proudly among the younger, inexperienced homes. Unafraid to show its weathered history, it commanded attention by having successfully survived the last two hundred years on this narrow spit of land.

I was excited to be there, and with good reason. During the tour, I learned about pirates, witches, ghosts, Native Americans, Civil War soldiers, a death by poisoning and even a ghost cat, all with ties to the house and land. I was hooked.

The house opened again on Tuesday, and I arrived bright and early for a history tour. As the guide was introducing herself, she looked at me and jokingly said, "I think you should start giving tours." I said, "Okay." She looked at me funny but continued with the tour. My fascination and interest only grew as I learned more about the history of the house. When the tour was over, I asked the guide if I could volunteer. She said yes, and I was back when they reopened on Thursday. I've never left.

Little did I know how much I would come to love and cherish not only this house but also its volunteers who so warmly welcomed me in. They have worked endlessly to keep Ferry Plantation well maintained and open for guests. And yes, I do now give tours!

I have never quite understood the connection I feel to the home. Another volunteer once told me that the house calls to the people it wants to be there. I believe that. Several mediums who have been on my tours have told me that I used to live there in another life. Maybe. But I came across a new term the other day that seems to pinpoint this feeling: *soul place*. In such a location, a person feels like they're home, sensing a strong connection and an overwhelming awareness of belonging. Ferry Plantation is my soul place.

And I am not alone. The house reaches out to many volunteers and guests alike who also experience this feeling of peace, connection and belonging. What is it that draws us in? The house? The history? The families who lived there? The land? The spirits?

I believe it's all of the above. You cannot separate one from the other. I have learned that trying to prove the existence of spirits requires more than readings on ghost hunting equipment. One needs to have an understanding of a location's history, a basic knowledge of the families who called this place home and a realization that tragic as well as happy events took place there. I believe that energy remains, and the spirits dwell within that energy. Every now and then, they happen to cross paths with the living. Maybe the spirits at Ferry Plantation have called the other volunteers and me to help maintain the house or to continue researching their families. I believe both to be true. But most importantly, I feel they have called us to tell their stories. As I spend time at the house, I wonder about the many lives that have passed through those rooms—who they really were, what they felt, what made them laugh and what made them cry. If those walls could talk! At Ferry Plantation, sometimes they do.

In this book, I hope to accurately portray each of our many spirits at Ferry as the people they once were. I have set this against the historical backdrop in which they lived. Each one is full of their own unique personality that still exists and defines them today, years after they passed from the physical world. They each had a life. They each have a story. I will share both in this book in the hopes of bringing them to life for you, whether it be through the historical record or through the spirit that remains. As my friend and fellow volunteer Joshua Husak says, even if you don't believe the house is haunted, who doesn't like a good ghost story?

Letter to the Reader

Ferry Plantation House has captured the imagination of Virginia Beach residents for generations. Its brick façade, made all the more unique because of a wing covered in whitewashed siding, begs people to tell stories about it. The house's connection to the city's history makes this impulse even stronger. At one point or another, a ferry, courthouse, jail and tavern operated on what was called Old Donation Farm, meaning Ferry Plantation House occupies land that was once at the center of Princess Anne County life. Since the house in its current form was built around 1820, it never served these public functions, but this reality never stopped locals from associating the house with the area's storied past. In particular, the bars that cover one of the windows on the ground floor have drawn the attention of visitors, making them contemplate a period when the county's accused and convicted criminals were jailed there. The fact that Grace Sherwood was tried for witchcraft and ducked nearby in 1706 has only enhanced the allure of this window. For more than a century, locals have claimed that it proves the supposed witch was imprisoned at Ferry Plantation.

When Admiral Lewis Walke toured the house in 1914, he heard this rumor from its owner. She told him that "neighborhood tradition says that the house was formerly the jail and courthouse of Princess Anne County, and one of the ground floor rooms, now used for a bathroom, is said to have been the jail, and Grace Sherwood, the famous Virginia witch, is said to have been incarcerated therein." When he recounted this story, he noted that he heard it while standing in front of the barred window of the former jail. More than a decade later, the *Virginian-Pilot* repeated this "neighborhood tradition" when it profiled Ferry Plantation. The article noted that "the kitchen wing of the house remains unaltered, and to this day the heavily barred windows of the little pantry mark the cell of the jail adjoining the courthouse where Grace Sherwood was confined in the year 1706. To stand within this dark, musty, incredibly tiny barricade is to experience a vivid sympathy with the prosaic matron who was accused of witchcraft." These rumors were still alive in the 1990s, when Ferry Plantation House faced an uncertain future as city leaders, real estate developers and preservation groups fought over what should be done with it. As the *Virginian-Pilot* covered these developments, it could not help but add that Ferry Plantation was "reputedly…haunted by Grace Sherwood, the Witch of Pungo, since she was locked in a cellar in 1706 where the house now stands."

Jo Howren, who lived in Ferry Plantation in the 1980s, was among those who claimed to see Sherwood's ghost, describing it as "young [and] slender, with long dark hair and wearing a long gown." Howren shared her experience at a civic league meeting in 1994 alongside others who recounted their own supernatural encounters. All of them lived on land that had once been part of Old Donation Farm, and their stories were in good company. Locals have been telling ghostly tales about Ferry Plantation for as long as they have been talking about the house itself. In fact, Emma Virginia Greenwell Ellis, who lived nearby in the early twentieth century, used to laugh as she recalled people "running out at night because there was a ghost in the house." Ferry Plantation's haunted history, which you are about to read, proves they were not alone in suspecting that there is more to the house than meets the eye.

While these stories are unique, they are part of the wider fascination people have with such spaces. Haunted houses are a ubiquitous part of American cultural life, and for good reason. In his book *Ghostland: An American History in Haunted Places*, author Colin Dickey explained that "stories of the dead [help us] to make sense of the living." In other words, they not only allow us to grapple with unnerving questions related to life, death and what comes after, but they also help us to come to terms with the challenges of our own lives. They allow us to realize that the struggles we face have been confronted before. They also help us to imagine our past. People often assume that historic houses, like Ferry Plantation, are haunted because they are uncanny reminders of our history. Even when they are well maintained and fully integrated into the communities around them, they still stand apart. They might be part of the modern world, but they also belong to a time gone by. As the stories recounted in this book demonstrate, it is hard to walk through houses like Ferry Plantation and not contemplate the people who were there in previous generations. The tales told about them ask listeners to do the same.

Such stories help create a sense of identity and form an important piece of a community's heritage. At the same time, their details and historical accuracy are often murky at best and impossible to prove. They are better thought of as pieces of historical memory—that is, the way we imagine our past—than as actual history, which requires verification from written sources. It would be a mistake, however, to dismiss these stories as trivialities. Because they are an important part of a place's identity, they are essential to its sense of self. Sharing them helps build a sense of community and allows people to feel more connected to their neighbors and those who have come before them. At the same time, it is important to see the line between history and legend and understand the difference between the two. This book does not just recognize this distinction—it gives readers the best of both worlds Kristen Ellis not only recounts the stories that people have shared about Ferry Plantation for generations, but she also provides a comprehensive look at the house's rich past. Reading it, you cannot help but understand why Ferry Plantation House is one of Virginia Beach's most beloved places.

—SCOTT O. MOORE
Author of *The Witch of Pungo: Grace Sherwood in Virginia History and Legend*

INTRODUCTION

When I am at Ferry, I first ask permission to enter as I am an intruder in its past. The house gives you a warm feeling even on the coldest day, and you feel welcome. The search for information on the families is always top priority because you get the longing from the house to find out more….

I can step into the past as well as many others that feel the same way about the house as I do.

I will always be sparked by the passion of the house….Many visitors come and go from the Ferry Plantation House each year, but when some leave, they have lasting memories they take with them….It could be at any time of the day when visiting the historic Ferry Plantation House. You enter any room and get that feeling that you are not alone. Shortness of breath, heaviness on your chest, signs that someone from the past is trying to contact you. I call those visitors "soul prints of the past." They just want their story told.

—*Belinda Nash*

I would never attempt to write a book on Ferry Plantation House without first introducing Belinda Nash. Originally from Ontario, Canada, Belinda moved to Virginia Beach in the early 1980s. Dedicating her time to researching local history, she began volunteering at Ferry Plantation in 1996. She quickly became instrumental in the house's preservation, restoration and opening of the home to the community through tours and special events. This affectionately earned her the nickname the "Duchess of Ferry Plantation House." As I have researched the house for the past five years, I'm always amazed to find such a variety of pictures of Belinda, from painting up on a ladder to teaching children during summer history camp or hosting ladies' teas in her finest colonial dresses. She led numerous fundraising events for Ferry, including Pumpkin Flings, themed teas and the Stroll of Lost Souls. Belinda was also instrumental in researching and sharing the story of Grace Sherwood, the infamous "Witch of Pungo." I discuss Grace Sherwood and Belinda's role in her story in the last chapter of this book. Additionally, Belinda coauthored three books on local history, ghost stories and this legendary witch. Her dedication to researching Ferry Plantation has been a tremendous inspiration to me as I continue to pursue her mission of sharing stories about this home and the families who lived there.

Belinda Nash, former director of Ferry Plantation, 2003. *Courtesy of the Friends of Ferry Plantation House.*

Unfortunately, I never had the opportunity to meet Belinda. She passed away in 2016, three years before I came to Ferry. From what I've heard from those who knew her best, once she set her mind to something, it was going to get done. It was through her strong will and perseverance that Ferry Plantation stands today, fully restored and open to share its rich history with anyone who passes through its doors.

Belinda surrounded herself with a team of dedicated volunteers who were on board with her mission to preserve and restore this important site in Virginia Beach history. I will discuss the home's restoration later, but a stipulation in saving the home was that everyone associated with Ferry be a volunteer, including the board of directors. Belinda, along with her committed team, gave their blood, sweat and tears to see Ferry transformed from a building marked for demolition to the beautiful historic home that still stands today.

Ferry Plantation would not be what it is now without the extraordinary efforts and dedication of the people who don't actually live there but call this place home. Throughout the book, I will share stories from the volunteers who work tirelessly to make sure that Ferry Plantation House is well managed, physically maintained and ready for guests to come learn more about this "Legacy on the Lynnhaven."

As you're reading through the history in this book, please know that this area of southeastern Virginia was originally known as Lower Norfolk

County. In 1691, Princess Anne County was formed. In 1963, the name changed once more to the modern-day City of Virginia Beach. Most of the history I discuss in this book takes place during the time when the area was known as Princess Anne County.

I mentioned earlier that I believe it's difficult to understand the spirits in a location without first knowing the history. I have designed each chapter of this book with the historical information at the beginning, and then I end with stories about our spirits that are associated with that particular period. I start with the sixteenth- and seventeenth-century history of the Lynnhaven River, including the ferry system, local Chesapeake Indians and pirates. The eighteenth century saw the building of the third Princess Anne County courthouse and, later, the majestic Walke Manor House. I show the transition of the property from the prominent Walke family to the McIntoshes, who hailed a fallen hero from the Civil War. At the turn of the twentieth century, we meet the Barnett family, who suffered a terrible loss in the home but lived there until the mid-1900s. The farm then changed hands to the Hudgins/Howren family, who called Ferry home until the early 1980s. A battle then began that resulted in saving and restoring Ferry Plantation House. This victory has allowed the home to play an important role in preserving and sharing local history.

Recent years have seen a marriage of historic places with the paranormal. Ferry Plantation is no exception. People have become excited to try out the newest ghost hunting equipment by staying up all night in supposedly haunted locations, hoping to catch proof of the afterlife. With a quick tap on our phones, we can get apps to let us know if a spirit may be near. Click another app, and it'll tell us what they are saying. Click another, and it will show us where they are standing. This ghostly world has even created its own language, as paranormal investigators can tell you the difference between an EVP, an SLS and a K2. We are glued to the TV as we watch our paranormal shows, straining to hear that voice, bump or knock. It has become a fascinating and popular pastime.

There is also a beneficial side to this ghost hunting attraction. Due to the fact that most of the paranormal hot spots are historic locations, the interest in the supernatural helps preserve local history by bringing in the funds necessary to maintain these important sites. As general interest declines in preserving historic places, the paranormal brings about a curiosity in the past that is ultimately saving and maintaining these irreplaceable landmarks. For nonprofit organizations like Ferry Plantation, we have more opportunities to not only share our spirits but also protect our rich cultural history.

I have spent countless hours in Ferry Plantation House, both alone and with others. I have experienced voices, footsteps, smells, touches, knocks and sighs, just to name a few. Sometimes the house is very active, while other times it's…well, rather dead. In my time there, I've often wondered what truly separates the living from those who have passed. Or perhaps the question should be, "What connects us?"

In the case of Ferry Plantation, I believe we are joined by the love and passion we share for this house. Some of the souls resided there, while others of us do not. Regardless, there is a strong sense of belonging. The house has called to each of us, bonding us together, bringing us home.

Room Names at Ferry Plantation

Kitchen: The modern kitchen beside the east side entrance.

Courthouse: The eastern wing of the house that served as a courthouse in the eighteenth century. It was later used as the kitchen for the Walke Manor House.

Loom Room: The room above the courthouse, currently displaying looms and examples of textiles. It formerly housed enslaved people and servants.

Henry's Room: Attic space above the Loom Room in the old courthouse section of the house. Home to Henry, an enslaved man from the nineteenth century.

Dining Room: Part of the first addition to the courthouse in 1830.

Breezeway: First-floor hallway connecting the front and back doors. Historically it served as a waiting area to greet guests when arriving at the house.

Library: This room served as an office, library and post office in the nineteenth century.

Best Parlor: The parlor located in the west wing of the house. It was used for entertainment and social gatherings. It was also known as the "death room" when used for wakes and funerals. This section was built in 1850.

Gift Shop: Historically served as the older boys' bedroom on the second floor.

Green Room: Historically served as the parents' bedroom on the second floor.

Conference Room: Historically served as the older girls' bedroom on the second floor.

Nanny's Room: A small room for the nanny located on the third floor by the nursery.

Nursery: A room that housed the children on the third floor.

Lynnhaven River

Maybe we're not watching ghosts so much…
but we're watching people from the past walk into our lives.
—Von Braschler

FERRYBOAT SYSTEM

In the wetlands of southeastern Virginia, a tidal estuary called the Lynnhaven River flows into the Chesapeake Bay. In 1642, before bridges were constructed, community leader Adam Thoroughgood established a ferryboat service on the river. The colonial courts had established early on that ferries were a public responsibility and were to be supported by a public tax because the roads that existed were little more than paths. Due to the jagged, extended shoreline of the Lynnhaven River, it could take days to reach a location on the opposite side. In this area of Princess Anne County, ferries were essential for transportation.

The ferry service provided an opportunity for commerce along the river. Thoroughgood created eleven stops, including one at Ferry Landing, where Ferry Plantation House sits today. Named for this water transit system, Ferry Plantation sits on a raised area of land, overlooking the Lynnhaven River. This spot was chosen as a stop because the land had already been cleared by the Chesapeake Indians in the 1500s. Another stop farther upriver, Two Penny Point, was so named because it cost a penny to ride the ferry each way.

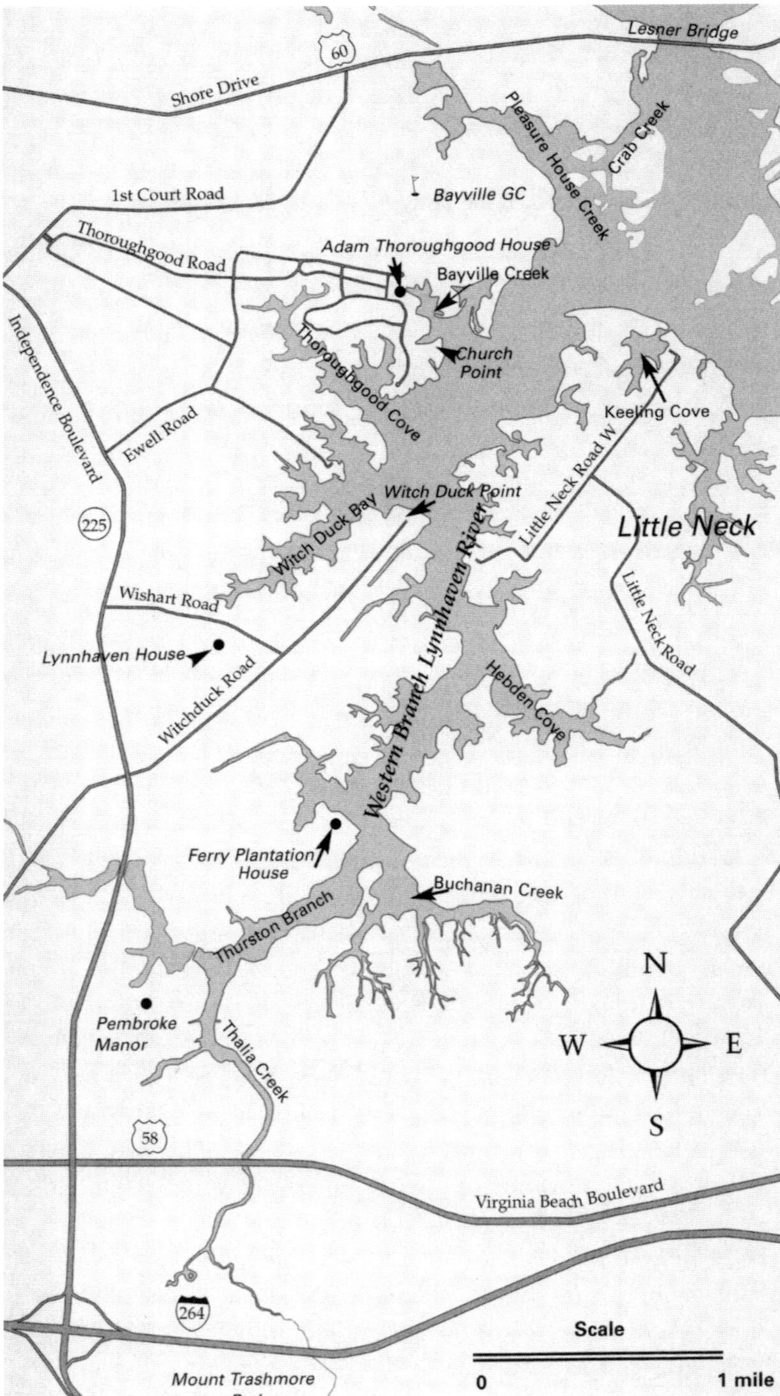
Lesner Bridge
60
Shore Drive
Pleasure House Creek
Crab Creek
1st Court Road
Bayville GC
Thoroughgood Road
Adam Thoroughgood House
Bayville Creek
Church Point
Thoroughgood Cove
Independence Boulevard
Ewell Road
Keeling Cove
Little Neck Road W
Witch Duck Point
Witch Duck Bay
225
Little Neck
Wishart Road
Little Neck Road
Lynnhaven House
Witchduck Road
Western Branch Lynnhaven River
Hebden Cove
Ferry Plantation House
Buchanan Creek
Thurston Branch
Pembroke Manor
Thalia Creek
N
W
E
S
58
Virginia Beach Boulevard
264
Scale
0
1 mile
Mount Trashmore Park

Opposite: Map of the Western Branch of the Lynnhaven River. *Courtesy of Vickie Shufer.*

Above: Ferry Plantation's replica ferryboat. *Author's collection.*

Thoroughgood hired a Frenchman named Saville Gaskins to operate the ferry. Gaskins was a colorful character who was hired to help pay off his court debts from charges of slander. In her book *Gateway to the New World*, Florence Kimberly Turner described Gaskins as having "an abundance of ambition but not enough common sense," as court records show that he continually stayed in debt. Records also show that he lived on the land known as Scull Neck, which is where the Lynnhaven House now stands.

As the ferry operator, Gaskins would be summoned to a particular ferry stop when he heard the firing of a small signal cannon. These were positioned at each of the eleven stops. Three of these cannons have been found along the banks of the Lynnhaven River. One was lost to the river, one crumbled when it was pulled to shore and the other has since disappeared.

The first ferries were simple skiffs rowed by men. They could hold several passengers, their goods and even a horse. Around 1720, larger skiffs were used to transport horse-drawn vehicles. The county later expanded the fleets to include six rowboats, each able to transport eight people, as well as three boats for wagons. These boats allowed farmers to take their produce to market more quickly. In an era before refrigeration, if a farmer wasn't able to get his crops to market in a reasonable amount of time, he would lose his harvest to rot. The Lynnhaven ferry system aided in the overall commercial prosperity of the area.

WINDMILL

Ferry Landing was an important stop for the Lynnhaven ferry because early settlers built a windmill on the land. Farmers would bring their wheat, corn and oats by boat, paying one bag for every five milled. The windmill that originally stood on the shore was built on skids and pulled inland so it wouldn't be destroyed if a storm approached. The sails were made of leather and lowered when not being used. Records show that the mill at Ferry Landing was a lucrative business in 1740. In 1996, the Friends of Ferry Plantation House searched the area along the river and found the remains of the trough dug to retain the tidal waters for the windmill. This area is now on private property.

One of the original Ferry Landing millstones is currently located at Ferry Plantation, sitting under the magnolia tree behind the house. It had remained on the property until the mid-1900s, when it was moved to another location in Virginia Beach. In October 2012, it was donated back to the house.

This millstone represents an important time in Ferry Plantation history. Rear Admiral Henry Walke recollected his childhood days in the early

Original millstone from the windmill at Ferry Landing. *Author's collection.*

The Robertson Windmill in Colonial Williamsburg represents the type of windmill that once stood at Ferry Landing. *Author's collection.*

nineteenth century in *Brief Records and Recollections of the Walke Family and Relations in the United States*. He wrote, "Another interesting object in the landscape was the lofty windmill, sweeping the clouds with its wings, as it seemed to us children when visiting there." He also made note on his return visit in 1826 that "the old wind-mill" was one of the few structures that remained on the farm. In 1853, Colonel Thomas Williamson painted the Ferry property and made sure to include this structure along the banks of the Lynnhaven River.

In her children's book *The Witch of Pungo*, Louisa Venable Kyle wrote about the Native Americans in the area when the windmills were first constructed. She described the loud noise made by the grinding millstones, terrifying and forcing the Native Americans to hide in the woods. Later, when they were shown the ground grain, they believed that there was an evil spirit living in the mill that ground up the grain with his teeth. She went on to explain the danger of working in the windmills, as an unexpected storm could cause increased wind, and the miller wouldn't be able to stop the turning of the millstones. All he could do was to continue to pour on more grain in hopes that a spark from the millstones wouldn't cause the structure to catch fire.

CHESAPEAKE INDIANS

The Chesapeake Indians were native to the area now known as Virginia Beach, occupying the land from the Atlantic Ocean to the Elizabeth River for more than two thousand years. The Chesapeakes were one of the Algonquian tribes, living along the banks of the saltwater and freshwater bays, rivers and marshes, eating small game, waterfowl, fish and shellfish. They used stone projectile points to hunt deer, although they had to trade for them as stone is not found near the coast. They also raised corn, tobacco, beans, pumpkins and squash. They sheltered in *yehakins*, which were houses made of saplings set in rectangles, bent and tied to the top, covered in bark or mats made of grasses and reeds. Village sites were located along the creeks and rivers, and the Chesapeakes used the waterways for transportation and communication.

In 1585 and 1587, English colonists John White and Thomas Hariott explored the area of what is now eastern North Carolina and Virginia. They were likely the first Europeans to cross into the land of the future Princess Anne County. On their journey, they encountered the Chesepiocs, spending the winter with them in 1585–86. They talked of the Chesapeake village of Apasus, located near the current-day Adam Thoroughgood House. They also visited the village of Chesepioc near Great Neck Point. John White later became well known for his detailed illustrations of these and other Native Virginia peoples.

During this period, the powerful chief Powhatan had established a confederacy that included more than thirty tribes from the Tidewater area of Virginia to the Potomac River farther north. Even though the Chesapeakes spoke the local dialect, they resisted becoming a part of Chief Powhatan's confederacy. In her book *The Powhatan Indians of Virginia*, Helen Rountree explained that Powhatan's priests told him that "from the Chesapeack Bay a Nation should arise, which should dissolue and guie end to his Empier." Powhatan concluded that the threat came from the Chesapeakes, and he ordered the entire tribe to be massacred. Rountree noted that "all the Inhabitants, the weroance and his subjects" were killed. Through what is now known as the Powhatan Prophecy, the Chesapeake tribe was completely obliterated. Ironically, it was soon after, in 1607, that three English ships "arose" out of the Chesapeake Bay and settled in Jamestown, America's first permanent English colony. Within just a few decades, due to warfare and disease, Powhatan's empire had collapsed, thus fulfilling the prophecy.

SPIRITS OF THE NATIVE AMERICANS

The Chesapeake Indians inhabited the land where Ferry Plantation now stands. Volunteers and neighbors have found dozens of arrowheads while gardening at Ferry and the surrounding land. In the 1990s, the Old Donation Farm neighborhood was built, and the Ferry Plantation House was to be torn down so a recreation center could be built in its place. Behind the house, the tennis court was built first. It is believed that it was built on top of a Chesapeake Indian burial ground because, it is told, as the construction workers dug up the land, they unearthed bones and arrowheads. The house was ultimately saved, but the tennis court remains. In the early years of the home's restoration, volunteers invited a local Native American tribal chief to come bless the land. He told them that there are many unsettled spirits—not just a few, but hundreds of spirits—in the area of the tennis court. According to the neighborhood myth, if anyone plays tennis or basketball on the court, they will likely twist or break their ankle.

Today, four hundred years later, the spirits of the Chesapeakes still occupy the land around Ferry Plantation. Guests on tours have reported hearing drums when they walk outside near the tennis court, even before they have been told about the Native American ties to the land. At other times, neighbors have called to complain that our drum circle is keeping them awake. They have called on nights when there aren't any events.

One of our volunteers, Cody Green, describes himself "as a hypersensitive. I see, hear, feel, and smell every day…and have done it all my life." At Ferry, Cody has seen the spirits of three Native Americans whom he refers to as Bear, Chief and Little Wolf. He described Bear as a "massive, big dude!" who protects the house from outside. He described Chief as being very

The tennis court behind Ferry Plantation House is believed to be built on top of a Chesapeake Indian burial ground. *Author's collection.*

much like a Native chief and appears more like a white shape. Little Wolf is very slight but a warrior. Cody said he sees Little Wolf and Bear the most. Chief mostly appears if something is wrong and he feels the need to protect the land. He is mostly seen on the tennis court.

Cody shared an experience he once had with the Native Americans. It was Family Night at Ferry, and he had arrived first. It was already dark, so he was waiting outside on the bench. He was watching the sky, seeing wolf heads appear in the clouds and hearing a drum circle from the direction of the tennis court. He zoned out and went into a trance. He described the experience as more vivid than a dream. He felt like he was living in that moment. He doesn't know who he was in the vision, but he was on the land where Ferry now stands. Of course, the house wasn't there. He realized that he was one of the Natives, yelling and fighting as they were under attack. Everyone around him was grabbing weapons. He was running to join the battle when he took an arrow in his left shoulder and in the side of his stomach. He dropped to the ground and was dragged away. When he woke up on the bench, he could still feel the pain. He firmly believes that he witnessed and took part in Powhatan's attack on the Chesapeakes. He explained that often events like this will happen on the anniversary of the event. Of course, we don't know what day the Chesapeakes were attacked, but he said that it can also happen when the energy is just right in the area.

In his book *Encounters with the Paranormal, Personal Tales of the Supernatural: Volume 4, Ferry Plantation Edition*, author Mike Ricksecker interviewed Julia Elliott, who also had an experience with the Native Americans at Ferry. She was staying in the house overnight with a paranormal team, and around 3:00 a.m., she was awakened to what felt like someone standing on her air mattress. As she fully woke up, she heard "what sounded like Indian flute music and drums coming from outside." She explained that maybe she was just very tired, but she could have sworn she also saw the light from a fire coming from the back of the property. Julia said that she went back to sleep and dreamed that she heard a woman's voice tell her, "Everything you see and feel about these spirits are true." She said that this was the most intense paranormal experience she'd ever had.

PIRATES ON THE LYNNHAVEN RIVER

The late 1600s began the golden age of piracy. We often think of the Caribbean when we think of pirates, but these notorious terrors of the seas were also commonly seen along the coasts of North Carolina and Virginia during the seventeenth century. They brought fear to not only the many ships transporting goods to and from Europe but also the coastal towns that were vulnerable to attack. In his book *Colonial Virginia's War Against Piracy: The Governor & the Buccaneer*, Jeremy Moss explained that in 1688, pirates were described as "traytors…thieves, robbers, murtherers, and confederates upon the sea…or in or upon any other haven, river, or creek." Some of the more notorious pirates were known to hide in the inland rivers so as not to be seen by traveling vessels in the Atlantic Ocean, manned by those who were trying to bring them to justice.

Two such pirates decided to tempt fate by sailing into the Lynnhaven River early in the eighteenth century. The first was French buccaneer Louis Guittar, who arrived at the mouth of the Lynnhaven River in April 1700. He commanded the ship *La Paix* (or *Peace*), a fourteen-gun swift ship of Dutch construction, which he had captured off the island of Tortuga. With the speed and firepower that *La Paix* afforded, Guittar plundered ships in the West Indies before turning to make his way to Virginia. When Guittar reached the waters of Virginia, he successfully captured five ships in the Lynnhaven Bay. He took prisoners, keeping them in the hold of *La Paix*.

When word of Guittar's exploits reached the governor of Virginia, action was taken. Virginia Governor Francis Nicholson, in preparation and expectation of a pirate invasion in the Chesapeake Bay, had just replaced the inefficient *Essex Prize* with the HMS *Shoreham*. Loaded with thirty guns, Governor Nicholson finally had a formidable ship to protect the waterways of coastal Virginia. With the powerful *Shoreham*, Governor Nicholson ordered Captain William Passenger to set out into the Lynnhaven and engage *La Paix*

Lynnhaven River. *Author's collection.*

in battle. Guitar fought under a blood-red flag, meaning the pirates would fight to the death and would show no mercy. The skirmish lasted six to eight hours. The *Shoreham* proved more powerful, and in the end, thirty-nine crew members of *La Paix* were killed. Moss wrote, "*La Paix* had disintegrated under the continuous pounding." It finally ran aground at Lynnhaven, and its lines were shot away. Guittar surrendered. They say that the waters of the Lynnhaven River ran red with blood that day.

Guittar surrendered, but not without first making a bargain. He told Governor Nicholson that he would blow up *La Paix* with its English prisoners

in the hold if he and his crew were to be immediately executed. Nicholson conceded to imprison the 124 pirates on board instead of executing them. They were to be sent to England for trial; 40 to 50 English prisoners were spared as a result of this agreement. There were, however, a few pirates who had escaped. John Hoogling leaped into the Lynnhaven and swam ashore, only to be captured. The other two, Cornelius Franc and François Delaunee, were found on a captured merchant ship. Since they were not on board *La Paix* at the time of the agreement, Nicholson decided that they were not subject to the same terms, and they would be tried for their crimes in Virginia. The three pirates were tried, convicted and ordered to be hanged. Florence Kimberly Turner wrote that the warrant for execution was sent to the court of Princess Anne County on May 17, 1700, with strict orders: "You must use cedar or other lasting wood, and leave him hanging in a good strong Chaine or Rope 'til they rott and fall away." Louis Guittar and his fellow pirates from *La Paix* were sent to London, tried, found guilty and executed on November 23, 1700.

Another pirate who frequented the waters of the Lynnhaven Bay may be more familiar to us. The notorious and perhaps most feared pirate of his time, Blackbeard, is said to have sailed into Lynnhaven Bay and buried some of his treasure around Lake Joyce and Cape Henry. His presence is still reflected today in the naming of areas in Virginia Beach: Blackbeard Road, Blackbeard's Island, Blackbeard Point, Treasure Island, Pirates Hill, Lookout Road and Pleasure House Road. Blackbeard, born as Edward Teach, earned his name from his braided black beard that reached down to his chest. He was famous for instilling fear by putting burning matches under his hat so that his face and head were ringed in smoke.

In her book *Gateway to the New World*, Florence Kimberly Turner wrote that in 1718, as ships along the North Carolina coast were being plundered by pirates, Blackbeard found an ally in North Carolina Governor Charles Eden. Eden pardoned Blackbeard in exchange for his loot to sell in Bath, North Carolina, where the governor was living at the time. The people of North Carolina complained about their ships being captured by pirates, but Governor Eden ignored them. They then turned to Governor Alexander Spotswood of Virginia. Spotswood was known to have a strong dislike of pirates, Blackbeard in particular. He became aware that Blackbeard was sailing to Ocracoke Island, North Carolina, to set up a base.

Spotswood sent two vessels to North Carolina: the HMS *Pearl* with thirty-five men under Lieutenant Robert Maynard and the HMS *Lyme* with twenty-five men under Midshipman Baker. They arrived in Ocracoke on November 21, 1718. Even though Blackbeard had been forewarned that these vessels were coming for him, he and his men spent the night partying and drinking. That didn't seem to affect his performance because when the battle began the next morning, Blackbeard immediately killed Baker and put the HMS *Lyme* out of commission. He then tied his ship to Maynard's, and his men came on board.

In what seems to have been an intensely dramatic confrontation, Maynard and Blackbeard found themselves face to face. Both men shot their guns. Blackbeard missed but Maynard did not. Blackbeard swung his cutlass and broke Maynard's sword in two. As he drew back for the final swing, Maynard's men shot the pirate and cut his throat. Blackbeard fell dead

Captain Teach, Commonly Called Blackbeard, circa 1734, by Joseph Nicholls. *Public domain.*

on the deck, having received twenty-five wounds, including five gunshots. Blackbeard's crew then surrendered. Legend has it that when Maynard ordered that they cut off his head, Blackbeard's body swam around the ship three times as if defying death. His head was then tied to the bowsprit and returned to Virginia, where it was delivered to Governor Spotswood.

Blackbeard's head was then hung on an iron pole in the coastal town of Hampton as a warning to other pirates venturing into the Chesapeake Bay. Legend also states that his head later became a popular drinking vessel in the taverns of Williamsburg.

Blackbeard seems to be as restless in death as he was in life. People claim to have seen his ghost at the site where his head once hung in Hampton. He appears in full pirate regalia, gripping a bloody cutlass, but is missing his head! Others claim to see only his ghostly head, eyes a bloody red and a tortured grimace on his face. The head floats along the ground as if searching for its body. In his book *Haunted Virginia Beach*, Alpheus Chewning explained how his high school English teacher told her students tales of Blackbeard. She explained that when the area suspected of housing Blackbeard's treasure was developed into First Landing State Park, prospectors would come and search the area for his loot. Even with heavy excavation equipment, no one ever found the treasure. According to local folklore, if anyone ever came close, the headless ghost of Blackbeard would appear and chase them away. It's said that he would then move his loot to another location. To this day, Blackbeard's treasure has never been found.

SPIRITS OF THE LYNNHAVEN RIVER

With such a rich and oftentimes tragic history of the Lynnhaven River, it's not surprising to hear that many locals claim to see or hear the spirits of some of those whose lives were claimed in this very water. More than several of these occurrences happened near Ferry Plantation.

In the seventeenth and eighteenth centuries, the Lynnhaven River was deep enough to support tall ships. In fact, it is believed that ships from England would often dock at Ferry Landing and unload their goods as a way to avoid the Crown's tax in Williamsburg. When the neighborhood was built around Ferry Plantation in the 1990s, a tunnel was discovered connecting the house to the water. The assumption is that this was used to hide and transport goods that were unloaded from the ships.

Cody Green recalled one particularly "crazy night all around" at Ferry. It was a beautiful night as he waited at the house for a paranormal team to arrive. He decided to walk down to the parking lot, and as he got closer, a strange fog appeared out of nowhere. He looked out toward the river and, to his amazement, saw a tall ship in the mist. He called another volunteer

Location of the eighteenth-century docks on the Lynnhaven River near Ferry Plantation House. *Author's collection.*

who was up at the house and asked her to hurry down to the parking lot. When she arrived, he asked her if she could see anything. She looked out at the river and said, "Is that a ship?"

Cody explained that the energy was ramped up that evening, but they couldn't figure out why. "Sometimes they like to party," he added. They watched the ship for a while, and as he looked at it, he felt all kinds of energy go by him, like people were walking by. He and the volunteer then turned to go back up to the house. When they did, they noticed wet footprints going all the way up the walk. When they arrived at the front door, there was a puddle, as if everyone was shaking off before entering the house.

During the evening, Cody kept feeling that they were having a party. Once the paranormal team arrived, they received the name "Virginia Dare" on their equipment, and the date corresponded to her birthday. Virginia Dare was the first child born in the New World to the settlers of the Roanoke Colony. These settlers are best known for their mysterious disappearance. They had been left in what is now coastal North Carolina while others sailed back to England for supplies. Three years later, when the supply ship returned, they found the colony abandoned. What happened to the colonists continues to be one of the area's greatest mysteries.

Cody felt that spirits had traveled to Ferry and gathered at the house that evening to celebrate Virginia Dare's birthday. The investigative team set up a portal (paranormal equipment that allows voices and sounds to come through) in the parlor. Immediately, they heard glasses clinking and conversations, as if a party was going on. At one point that evening, one of the investigators asked, "Should we fear death?" A voice responded from the portal, "She thinks we're dead!"

Later that evening, Cody stepped outside for a few minutes. As he was coming back into the house, he heard through the portal, "Is Cody still here?" He asked, "Did that thing just say my name?" They told him that it had said his name three times since he stepped outside. He said that was "one of the craziest nights I've ever had out there."

Others have also experienced supernatural occurrences in the area surrounding the river. In the YouTube video "Ferry Plantation, Haunted or Not? You Decide," Belinda Nash told a story that her neighbor Mrs. Stanley shared with her. She told her that back in 1734, they were building a bridge that crossed the Lynnhaven River from Ferry Plantation over to the Glebe Land (church property). One day during this construction, a pile of cypress pilings fell and entrapped a young enslaved boy underwater. The only way to free him was to cut off his leg. Mrs. Stanley, a family descendant of this child, claimed that his screams could still be heard when she used to come down to the water and sit on the dock. She said the screams would become so loud that she couldn't stand it any longer and had to leave. She lived to be 96 years old and always claimed that the screams came from her enslaved relative who had died there more than 250 years earlier.

In 2003, Belinda recorded that another neighbor claimed to hear ships being unloaded at the pier. She asked Belinda if they always unloaded at night. "No," Belinda replied, "not in over a hundred years!" There have been reports from other neighbors hearing the sounds of water splashing against heavy timbers as if ships were still anchored in the river. They claim to hear the clanking sound of chains associated with unloading cargo. The sounds of a busy waterfront along with indistinct voices make their way into the neighborhood, although no such ships have been anchored there for more than a century.

There is a theory in the paranormal world that water is a conduit for spiritual energy. Could this explain why so many spirits reside at Ferry Plantation House, with the home being located so close to the Lynnhaven River? Could it explain why there are so many ghost stories about pirates and the Native Americans who used this waterway as an integral part of their daily lives? Like the land surrounding Ferry Plantation, the Lynnhaven River harbors its secrets and mysteries. It has its own stories to tell.

Courthouse and Walke Manor House

The boundaries which divide life from death are at best shadowy and vague. Who shall say where the one ends and where the other begins?
—Edgar Allan Poe

Princess Anne County Courthouse

In the mid-1600s, the most prominent and important buildings of the early Virginia colony were located along rivers since traveling by water was the easiest means of transportation. The British Crown also wanted churches and courthouses close together since the church vestrymen often served as the court justices or jurors. According to this tradition, the first courthouse and 1st Lynnhaven Parish church in Princess Anne County stood in the area of current-day Church Point, located on the banks of the Lynnhaven River. After the river was diverted for an easier route to the Chesapeake Bay, this area flooded, and the church and courthouse were relocated in 1692. The second county courthouse stood next to the 2nd Lynnhaven Parish, near where Old Donation Episcopal Church stands today. In 1735, the third Princess Anne County Courthouse (and first one made of brick) was built at Ferry Landing. It served as a courthouse until 1751. During this time, Anthony Walke I served as the judge and held court there the first Wednesday of each month. The small, two-story, two-room courthouse mostly heard cases regarding debts, land transfers and caring for orphaned children. Cases were

Above: The third Princess Anne County Courthouse, which is now the eastern wing of the Ferry Plantation House. *Author's collection.*

Opposite: Bars still remain on one of the windows in the courthouse section of the Ferry Plantation House. *Author's collection.*

heard in the room downstairs, while the jury sat upstairs, out of view of any neighbors or family who might be on trial. This early Princess Anne County Courthouse is now the east wing of the Ferry Plantation House.

The most obvious sign that this part of the house served as a courthouse is the bars that are still on one of the downstairs windows. The rumor is that the Witch of Pungo, Grace Sherwood, was tried and jailed in this courthouse; however, this structure was not built until thirty years after her trial. (You can read more about the life and trials of Grace Sherwood in the chapter dedicated to her in this book.) There is, however, evidence that prisoners may have been held in a cellar room under the main courthouse. The space is only about four feet tall and has a dirt floor, but there is evidence of a fireplace. Fireplaces were built only in living areas. This holding cell area collapsed during the 1990s renovations of the house, making it no longer accessible. The first floor of the courthouse was replaced during the renovation, but the upstairs floor is original. Dendrochronological tests were conducted, showing that the wood from this floor dated back to the eighteenth century.

During this time, justice was quick and immediate, so if you were convicted of a crime punishable by death, you were dealt with immediately. Therefore, it was required that every courthouse have a mature hanging tree on the property. Lawyers, who were normally just well-educated, respected men but not trained in the law, didn't file for appeals and prolong the punishment. If you were deemed guilty, then you were perceived to be a threat to the community and would be put to death right away. A few hundred feet behind Ferry Plantation House stands a three-hundred-year-old sycamore tree, believed to be the original hanging tree. It would have been planted by 1700 to be mature enough to serve this purpose. If you put your head into the trunk, you can see all the way through to the top. We know that the tree has been struck by lightning at least three times since the 1960s, but still, it lives and thrives. An arborist visiting the house once told us that the tree knows it's supposed to be there. The tree has some odd features like several branches bent at right angles, which aren't normal in nature, and there is even one branch that has grown into a loop. That doesn't happen unless a branch is trained and molded to do so. Perhaps the most interesting feature is that new roots grow perpendicular to the main roots, resting on top of the older roots as if they are holding down the tree. One even has three mysterious smaller branches sprouting out of the end, which give it the illusion of a hand.

In the eighteenth century, Virginia had a rule that each county could have one tavern, but it had to be built beside the courthouse. There were several reasons for this. In her book *Gateway to the New World*, Florence Kimberly Turner explained that the justices of the court were "well-provided with drink, and all workers received their allotted 'pint' a day." Court day was a very important day in the county, not only for those attending court but also for merchants who came to sell their wares. This was a day of community gathering where neighbors and families socialized after not seeing one another since the previous month. With the only means of travel being

The hand-like root on the sycamore tree that is believed to have served as the hanging tree for the eighteenth-century Princess Anne County Courthouse. *Author's collection.*

by foot, boat or horse, many townspeople had long, arduous journeys to court that could take up to several days. The tavern was available for these overnight guests and offered stables for their horses. The tavern keeper also provided food and drink for all who had come for court day.

Records show that Anthony Walke, the judge, also owned the tavern that stood beside the courthouse. We don't find much surviving information on this "Walke Tavern," other than an advertisement for an "ordinary keeper" placed in the *Virginia Gazette* in 1739 by Anthony Walke himself. However, we do have archaeological evidence from the tavern. In 1987, before the Old Donation Farm neighborhood was built on the land surrounding Ferry Plantation House, archaeologists from Colonial Williamsburg conducted a dig on the site believed to be the tavern. According to an article from the *Virginian-Pilot* on July 9, 1987, "18th Century Artifacts Found at Ferry Farm," pewter spoons, wine bottles, ceramics and even a Spanish coin were found. Close to fifty thousand artifacts were removed from the site, proving to be the largest number of artifacts ever recovered from any colonial excavation at that time in Virginia.

THE WALKE FAMILY AND MANOR HOUSE

The courthouse at Ferry Landing was in service until 1751, when it was moved to the Newtown area of Princess Anne County. At this time, Ferry Landing and the surrounding property belonged to the prominent Walke family. In 1662, Thomas Walke I came to Lower Norfolk County (the county name until 1691). He came from Barbados, where his family had a thriving shipping business. Originally from Scotland, the Walke family decided to expand their business ventures into the new British colonies. Once established in this New World, he married into the prosperous Lawson family, became a local justice and church vestryman and acquired a substantial amount of land, making him one of the wealthiest men in Lower Norfolk County. In Rear Admiral Henry Walke's *Brief Records and Recollections*, he wrote that family tradition says that Thomas Walke I was known to "have been remarkable for his mild and gentle deportment, and when he was on his first voyage across the Atlantic, frequently chided the sailors for their profaneness, and entreated them to observe a more Christian conduct."

Thomas Walke's son, Anthony Walke I, was born on November 8, 1690. Like his father, he rose to a state of prominence in the Princess Anne County.

He served as a church warden of the 1st Lynnhaven Parish, a member of the House of Burgesses, judge of the Princess Anne County Court and tavern owner and acquired thousands of acres of land across the county. As a successful merchant, he also had stores in the developing city of Norfolk and engaged extensively in coastal and West Indian trade. He was deeded land (in what is now the Kempsville area of Virginia Beach) where he built his family mansion, Fairfield, in the mid-1700s. Anthony Walke imported brick from England for this impressive home. Rear Admiral Henry Walke described the house as a "baronial establishment on an extensive land-estate, distinguished for its retinue of liveried black servants, and the hospitality and splendor of its entertainments." The house was said to have four-feet-thick walls, and the interior walls and ceilings were decorated with wainscoting of black walnut. In her book *Lost Virginia Beach*, Amy Waters Yarinske shared the story of an old Princess Anne County farmer, John Ivy Herrick, who died in 1931. Herrick remembered visiting the house as a child and described how Fairfield had an exceptionally large parlor. He said that the family coat of arms hung over a hand-carved mantelpiece in the dining room. The Walke coat of arms features a buck's head with lofty antlers amid various crosses. It's no coincidence that a buck's head hangs in the parlor of Ferry Plantation House today. Sadly, the Fairfield manor house burned down on a windy March day in 1865.

Tomb of Anthony Walke I at Old Donation Episcopal Church. *Author's collection.*

The Walke family established a trusted and respected reputation among the citizens of Princess Anne County. Rear Admiral Henry Walke went on to say that the Walkes "were distinguished not only for wealth and hospitality, but as men of education, liberality, and piety." Anthony Walke I was first buried at Fairfield, but his grave was later moved to Old Donation Episcopal Church when the Fairfield plantation was sold to developers in the early 1970s. Walke had this church built at the Ferry at his own expense. His tomb stands out among the other graves in the Old Donation graveyard, as it is a raised tomb, adorned by square, striated columns in the corners and in the middle of the crypt. The scripted engraved writing has long since become illegible, but a plaque has been placed on top of the stone slab that reads:

To the Memory of Coll. Anthony Walke
a sincere Friend and cheerful Companion
Steady in the practice of Christianity
and a Zealous promoter of Virtue
he was for many Years a Member
of the House of Burgesses
and Judge of the Court of this County
In his public capacity he behaved himself
with a Uniform regard to Justice
tempered with mercy and in all respects
consulted the interests of the County
over which he presided.

he died the 8th day of November 1768
in the 76 Year of his Age

Anthony Walke II was born on January 3, 1726. Like his father and grandfather, he served as a vestryman at Old Donation Church. He was also part of the local militia and a member of the House of Burgesses and served on the Committee of Safety that enforced the ban on goods from England during the American Revolution. He is said to have turned in large amounts of his own English china during this time. Rear Admiral Henry Walke described his great-grandfather by saying:

Anthony Walke was a man of high standing and character. He was a Colonel and Commander of the troops of Princess Anne County, under his majesty King George III, but when the trouble with England began, he

> *espoused the cause of the colonies, and united with Patrick Henry, Mason, Madison, Marshall, Jefferson, and other patriots in resisting British oppression and in establishing American Independence.*

In the 1762 will of Anthony Walke II, he bequeathed the Ferry plantation to his son, William. He stipulated that if there wasn't already a dwelling house when his son became of age, one was to be built with a kitchen, laundry, smokehouse, dairy and other necessary outbuildings. In 1782, William Walke built a grand manor house at the Ferry. This home was larger than the one at Fairfield and built in a more modern English style. The two-story brick mansion stood on the Western Branch of the Lynnhaven River. The small brick courthouse now served as the kitchen for the Walke Manor House. According to the Mutual Assurance Society of Virginia's policy for the "Ferry Plain" of 1815, the house measured sixty feet by forty feet and was valued at $7,500. The only known image of the original house is a watercolor of the Ferry and its plantation, painted by General Thomas Hoomes Williamson in the mid-nineteenth century. Williamson was born in this home in 1813.

The Walke family grew tobacco as a source of income and currency in the eighteenth century. They had grown tobacco in Barbados but quickly learned that the tobacco grown in Virginia had a sweeter taste that was desired by England and other parts of Europe. This new form of tobacco was introduced by John Rolfe in the early 1600s. Rolfe would later marry Chief Powhatan's daughter, Pocahontas.

By the early nineteenth century, the Walkes had expanded their landholdings to nearly seven thousand acres of land across Princess Anne County. Unfortunately, growing tobacco depletes the soil of nutrients, and the Walkes were not able to sustain its production. It was at this time that one line of the Walke family moved to Chillicothe, Ohio, built a new manor house and continued to prosper in their new community. The manor house on the Lynnhaven River now stood mostly empty. It was used as a summer house or for special occasions. One such occasion, unfortunately, led to the destruction of the grand mansion. On September 12, 1828, it is said that a nephew was hosting a party, and amid the whiskey and cigars, someone knocked over an oil lamp, setting fire to the massive manor house. The fire is said to have reached a vat of whale oil in the basement, and the entire house exploded. People claim to have heard it all the way in Norfolk. The salvageable bricks from the manor house were later added onto the old courthouse to build the Ferry Plantation House that stands today.

Left: Portrait of Anthony Walke II. *Courtesy of the Princess Anne County/ Virginia Beach Historical Society.*

Below: Sign at the Ferry Plantation House. *Author's collection.*

The history of the Walke family would not be complete without mentioning Reverend Anthony Walke III. Half brother to William Walke, Reverend Walke was the first son of Anthony Walke II. His mother, Jane Randolph, was Anthony II's first wife, but she died several years into their marriage. Anthony Walke III, born in 1755, was their only child. Anthony II later married Mary Moseley, who gave birth to William. Reverend Anthony Walke III grew up to be an Episcopal minister and preached at Old Donation Church, as well as various other churches and chapels in Princess

Walke family graves at Old Donation Episcopal Church. *Author's collection.*

Anne County. During this time, people met at church to discuss politics and to see what the parson had to say on these matters. Generally, they followed his advice. In 1770, Reverend Walke was a member of an association, consisting of members of the House of Burgesses and leading merchants, that organized to resist the Stamp Act and other repressive measures pushed down on the colonists by the Crown. One of his biggest accomplishments was serving as a member of the Virginia Convention of 1788, which ratified the U.S. Constitution. He attended this event with his cousin Thomas Walke IV of Upper Wolfsnare Plantation.

Reverend Anthony Walke III was perhaps best known for his love of fox hunting. In her book *The History of Eastern Shore Chapel and Lynnhaven Parish, 1642–1969*, Louisa Venable Kyle recounted this humorous habit of Reverend Walke:

> *There is a delightful story handed down about the Reverend Anthony Walke who with great solemnity and in a mild clear voice read the word of life in this venerable sanctuary. But should he pause and the sound of horn and cry of hounds be heard during any part of the service, down got Parson Walke from the high pulpit and out of the chancel, mounting his horse which he kept tied in the church yard and was off after the fox with the best of them, leaving the Clerk, Mr. Dick Edwards, to finish the service.*

The prominent Walke family were instrumental in establishing the societal, religious and political foundation of Princess Anne County during the eighteenth century. The only remaining Walke family home from the 1700s is the Upper Wolfsnare House, built in 1759. It is currently owned and maintained by the Princess Anne County/Virginia Beach Historical Society. Standing as a true testament to the influence and fortitude of the Walke family, it is open for special events and well worth a visit.

SPIRITS IN THE COURTHOUSE OF FERRY PLANTATION

I am sitting in the downstairs courthouse room at Ferry Plantation as I'm writing this. There was just a noise from upstairs and a tapping on the window. When I came into this room a few minutes ago, I walked across tape that is on the floor, alerting people to a step. It's curling up on the edges, so it sticks to your shoe when you walk on it. Once I was fully in the room, the tape continued to make a sticking sound, as if other people came into the room after me.

When the house was restored, they rebuilt the courthouse fireplace in its original position. One of its features is a small brick oven. We show guests where bread was made for the prisoners that were housed below. There is a heavy wooden block that seals the oven, and it often gets so wedged in that it's nearly impossible to pull out. On several occasions, we have come in to find this wooden block on the floor across the room. If it were to just fall, it would be found in front of the fireplace. However, we usually find it some eight feet away from the hearth, sitting in the middle of the room.

We often have psychic mediums who come to the house, either on tours or with paranormal groups. We've had two psychic mediums, years apart, tell us how spiritually busy this courthouse room is. They get a sense of many people coming and going. In 2013, Sherry Baier stated that a lot of people sat around the fireplace and talked. She also sensed a "nice woman with good energy" sitting in a rocking chair by the window. This had been her favorite room. She would sit by the window and wait for her traveling husband to return home. She felt this woman had four children.

In the YouTube video "Ferry Plantation, Haunted or Not? You Decide," one of the volunteers explained how she and another girl were in the kitchen and walked into the courthouse. They witnessed two cups, normally sitting on butter churns, suspended in midair before they came crashing down to the floor. In this same video, other volunteers explained how one morning when they opened the house, they found wads of cotton and hay scattered

The wooden block from the brick oven in the courthouse fireplace is often found across the room. *Author's collection.*

throughout the courthouse and up the stairs. I want to point out that there are no cotton or hay fields around Ferry anymore.

In the upstairs of the courthouse, which we call the Loom Room, we have a few animal pelts because we talk about the Chesapeake Indians. One morning, when I went upstairs to turn on the light, I found a rabbit pelt, perfectly placed and smoothed out in the middle of the floor. It was a good three to four feet from where it normally hangs on the stair rail.

I was giving a tour one afternoon, and when we came down the stairs into the courthouse, we all heard a voice. Everyone stopped and looked at me. None of us could tell what was said, but each one of us clearly heard it. Another time, I came down the steps first and as I stood waiting for the group, there was a tug on my skirt. I thought I was stepping on it because the colonial skirts we wear are very long. I checked, but I wasn't standing on it. When I walked into the dining room immediately afterward, I felt the tug again. I figured it was one of the spirit children, trying to get my attention.

When we enter Ferry, we use a side door that comes into a short hall. On the right, there is a small modern kitchen, and on the left is a bathroom. One day, I was working in the kitchen when I heard a loud slam at the side door. I first thought another volunteer was coming in with their hands full and hit the door with their shoulder. But the sound seemed too loud for that. I came into the entry hall but didn't see anyone at the door. I went outside and looked around, but no one was there. I checked to see if anything fell in the bathroom. Everything was in its place. I then walked upstairs to look in the Loom Room, and all was exactly where it should be. Perplexed, I thought maybe a bird had flown into the door. Later that night, I checked the security video, and indeed, there was a loud bang at the door. I could see there was no one at the door when it happened, and the sound was too loud for it to have been a bird. To this day, I have no idea what caused it.

THE SPIRIT OF HENRY

When the middle section of the Ferry Plantation House was built in 1830, the upstairs and attic space above the old courthouse became the indoor slaves' and servants' quarters. We know enslaved people worked the land, as their names are listed in the estate records for Fairfield and

Ferry Plantations. As the volunteers at Ferry come across the names of these enslaved people, we engrave them on a brick and place them in the walkway of the necessary garden.

One of our best-known spirits at Ferry Plantation is Henry. Henry was a former slave on the plantation and continues to inhabit the attic space above the courthouse. The story is told that Henry was born on the plantation and was a young man at the time of the manor house fire. He was credited with saving the family and guests from the flames so was always well thought of and respected by the Walke family. At the end of the Civil War, when the enslaved people were freed, it's said that Henry was an old man and decided to stay on. He lived out the rest of his years at Ferry, making the attic space his home. Several years ago, when one of our volunteers was scraping off years' worth of paint in the upper courthouse room, she started yelling! Everyone ran up to see what happened, and she showed them what she found. Carved into the door frame leading up to Henry's room was the letter "H." Maybe it was the only letter Henry knew, but he seemed to be letting everyone know that was his space. Whenever I go up into Henry's room, I always ask him first if I can come up. This was his personal space, and I want to be respectful of that.

Ferry Plantation House was inhabited until the early 1980s. A caregiver used to come and stay when the last resident of Ferry moved to assisted living. It is said that during these times, the caregiver would sit by the courthouse window in the mornings and drink his coffee. On more than one occasion, he witnessed an African American man come into the room through the side wall, walk over to the oven, kneel down and work on something with his hands. The man would then stand, look at the caregiver, nod and then disappear back through the wall. What the caregiver didn't know, and what wasn't discovered until the house was renovated, was that the original

Opposite: Names of the enslaved workers at the Walke plantations. *Author's collection.*

Above: The engraved "H" on the door frame going to Henry's Room. *Author's collection.*

fireplace stood behind the modern oven. It was likely that Henry was in charge of keeping the fire going, so he was going about his morning routine just as he had been doing for the past hundred years.

When paranormal investigators come to the house, they often interact with Henry. Many have recorded him saying that he likes to go fishing. The Old Donation Farm neighborhood was built around Ferry in the 1990s, and some of the neighbors have reported having experiences with this spirit. The most common claim is that they wake up in the morning to find that their deck furniture has been moved during the night. When reviewing their security video, they have reported that the furniture moves by itself, often pulling to one side as if to create a path. Our theory is that Henry is walking down to the river to go fishing, and their furniture happens to be in his way. I heard that one neighbor actually moved as a result of these unexplained occurrences.

Earlier, I mentioned the tunnel that connected the house to the Lynnhaven River. It's speculated that Henry used to help unload the ships and would use the tunnels to transport goods up to the house. No one would think it strange that he made frequent trips to the river because he often fished. Belinda Nash noticed that the neighbors whose furniture was moved lived in houses that stood between Ferry and the old bridge that used to connect to the Glebe Land across the Lynnhaven River. Maybe Henry was heading there when he moved their furniture out of the way.

In his book *Encounters with the Paranormal*, Mike Ricksecker wrote about the time when he and his team first arrived at Ferry Plantation for an event and were given a tour of the house. As they were walking up the stairs to the Loom Room, they were hit by a strong, pungent fish smell. The guide said that she had never smelled that before in the house. Was this the smell of oysters that were often gathered and prepared in the house in the early 1900s? Or could this be a phantom smell from the fish Henry caught?

We feel that Henry is very much the protector of the house. One summer, when workers were putting in a new A/C unit outside, they called us to ask who the slave reenactor was who kept staring at them but wouldn't say anything. At that time, we didn't have any such reenactors. Henry is also known to stand behind guests on tours who may have bad intentions in coming to the house. He will close his eyes and bow his head. Our volunteer Cody is able to see him, and this is how Henry lets him know if there is someone to keep an eye on. A frequent guest to the house has mediumship abilities, and one day, she saw Henry standing behind one of our volunteers. He told her to tell this volunteer that he was there to protect us.

Lantern in Henry's Room. *Author's collection.*

A hot spot for paranormal activity is in the attic, or as we call it, Henry's Room. Investigators have captured voices, movements and shadows and have even felt someone touch them. One of our volunteers was helping to open the house for tours one day, and when opening Henry's door to turn on the lights, he said, "Hi Henry!" A voice upstairs responded, "Hi!" In his book *Encounters with the Paranormal*, Mike Ricksecker shared an experience from Brennan Guenzel, who was investigating in Henry's Room with two other people. As they talked, the discussion turned toward religion. One of the investigators said he didn't believe in heaven or hell. Suddenly, a K2 meter that was sitting on a box in the middle of the room went flying off the box and hit the brick wall. They teased the investigator, saying that they bet he believed now.

Several mediums have picked up on a young boy in Henry's Room. At least two have said that the little boy is "lame." One picked up on moaning and felt there was an infection in his right leg. In her 2022 visit, Ambrosia Matthews said he is scared when people come up to the attic, and he cowers in the corner. She picked up on a name that starts with "Ch." While researching the house, I found a list of Henry's brothers in a historical record from December 1842. He did have a brother named Charles. Could it be that Henry is still taking care of and protecting his brother after all these years? In 2013, Sherry Baier picked up on a family of slaves in Henry's Room. She felt they were treated well. She said she felt that even when Henry was an old man, he would still jump up and do things to help the family.

From people who have seen Henry, we know that he was a very large man. The attic seems to be proof of this, as the first crossbeam is missing as you come up the stairs. Being a tall man, he would've hit his head on this, so we assume he was the one who removed it. Another interesting aspect about the attic is that on many of the pine boards that form the underside of the roof, you can see fingerprints. We know that enslaved people would have built this attic space when the center section of the house was added in 1830. There was an oil they used when hammering in the nails, and this oil would've

Above: Fingerprints, believed to be from enslaved workers, remain on the ceiling planks in Henry's Room. *Author's collection.*

Left: Stairs leading up to Henry's Room. *Author's collection.*

gotten on their fingers. It's chilling to see the hands that actually built this room nearly two hundred years ago. The interesting thing is that when they started renovating the house in 1996, the earlier volunteers claimed that the fingerprints were not there. They only appeared later after the work on the house had begun.

I had never experienced anything paranormal in Henry's Room until the evening of a Friday the 13th event in October 2023. I was running around, gathering what we needed for the event, and I ran upstairs to get a basket. I threw open the door to Henry's Room to go into the attic, and what I saw stopped me in my tracks. The attic is unfinished, so there is a thick white industrial electrical cord that runs along the back of one of the stairs and into a lightbulb on the side wall. When I opened the door, that stiff cord was completely curved out and away from the step, suspended in midair! It stayed like that for a few seconds and then dropped, making the rest of the cord ripple over to the light. My first thought was that the suction from opening the door pulled it out, but that room is not airtight. You can look through the slats and see the light from the adjoining room. My next thought was that I had just scared a ghost. I felt like a spirit was on the steps, playing with the cord, and I startled them when I quickly opened the door. Is it possible to scare a ghost? I think I may have done just that.

THE GLIDING LADY

It seems that every haunted house has a Lady in White. Ferry also has one, but we refer to her as the Gliding Lady. Many have claimed to see a lone woman gliding in or around the Ferry Plantation House. She is described as thin with long hair, wearing a white gown that reaches the ground. She has been seen walking across the front and back of the house. One of the first descriptions of an encounter with this mysterious spirit comes from Belinda Nash, Lillie Gilbert and Deni Norred-Williams in their book *Ghosts, Witches & Weird Tales of Virginia Beach*. A caregiver living in the house in the 1980s described his experience. He claimed that while he was sitting in front of a fire in the den, a transparent woman came from behind him. He only saw her back:

> *She was wearing a long, flowing one-piece kind of dress, kind of flowy. What was also weird was her color. She was whitish, transparent looking.*

> *It caught me totally off guard and I'd say I didn't detect any steps, like someone walking. It was more like she kind of wisped on by.*

In Marlene Ford's 1999 article "Civic League Mulls Ferry Farm Ghost," a visitor described a paranormal experience that could be the Gliding Lady. Jo Howren, who was married to one of the last residents of Ferry, said that one night "it was pitch black outside, and I was fixing dinner in the kitchen. Grace came out of the dining room, past me and into the pantry door. She was young, slender with long, dark hair and wearing a long gown." Howren believed she saw Grace Sherwood, who was tried as a witch through a witch ducking in the nearby Lynnhaven River. But her description also closely matches that of the Gliding Lady. The pantry door that she went through used to be a second doorway to the dining room before it was closed off to make a pantry. In this same article, a prospective buyer of the house explained that when they were viewing the house, her nine-year-old daughter came running downstairs, saying that there was a lady in her room and she was worried she would have to share a room with her. The mother also had similar experiences with a "very young, very sad girl with long hair."

In the same article, one of the neighbors explained how frequently they would wake up in the morning to find all their deck chairs off the deck and in the grass. Mysteriously, they were all in a line facing the Ferry house. They also shared the story of how one night they both woke up at 2:00 a.m. "to see a young woman in a long, flowing gown with long hair walk out of their closet and across the room."

Nash, Gilbert and Norred-Williams described an additional witness experience from the Ferry parking lot:

> *There before my very eyes a form appeared in the shape of a woman in a long flowing white gown....I felt as if she wanted me to see her because she looked over the porch of the neighboring house, walked away, then returned to the edge of the porch, turned, and walked away again. I noted that she seemed to be gliding rather than walking.*

This last account caught my attention. Last fall, Cody and I were at the house one night with a paranormal group. There was a full moon, so at one point during the early hours of the morning, several members of the team went to sit outside on the back porch. While they were sitting there, they said a neighbor walked out of her house and crossed in front of them. She was wearing a long white nightgown. She told them that she had wanted to come out to see the full moon. Without saying anything else, the team continued to talk among themselves, not paying attention to where the lady went afterward. When they came in, they told us about this, saying it was rather odd that this woman would come out at that late hour. They also found it strange that once she saw them, she didn't turn to go back into her house, realizing that she was only wearing her nightgown. One of the ladies said, "You know, she didn't really walk. It was more like she glided." At this time, I hadn't yet heard the stories about the Gliding Lady, so I didn't put the thought in their heads beforehand. However, the more they talked, the more confused they became about this curious woman. I had them describe her to me, and she didn't match the description of the lady living in the house they said she came out of. It was a mystery and a bit unnerving to the team members who experienced this. I remember that for one lady in particular, every time I saw her during the remainder of the night, she had this perplexed look on her face and kept asking everyone, "What did we really see?"

General Thomas H. Williamson

The only image we have depicting the original Ferry Plantation is a painting of the Walke Manor House. While a Walke family descendant owns the original, a copy hangs above the mantel in Ferry's dining room. The curious thing is that it was painted as an aerial view of the Ferry house and plantation in 1853. The painting predates any modern means to obtain a view from above, like airplanes or drones. In spite of this, it is surprisingly accurate as far as the land and river features. General Thomas Hoomes Williamson created this watercolor from memory. The painting shows the house, Old Donation Church, the windmill, an orchard, outbuildings including the old courthouse/kitchen and two rows of tall cedar trees. One of these trees still stands by the Ferry Plantation House today. Williamson painted the watercolor twenty-five years after the house burned down. He was born in the original manor house in 1813, but his immediate family had sold it to relatives before the fire destroyed it in 1828. Thomas Williamson was the great-grandson of Anthony Walke II. His father, also Thomas H. Williamson, married into the family through Anne McClelland McCauley Walke.

The painting of the Walke Manor House by Thomas H. Williamson is the only visual representation we have of the original eighteenth-century house that stood at Ferry Plantation. *Author's collection.*

Thomas H. Williamson (Jr.) was a professor of practical engineering architecture and drawing at the Virginia Military Institute in Lexington, Virginia, in the 1850s. He also served under Stonewall Jackson during the Civil War. In *Brief Records and Recollections*, Rear Admiral Henry Walke remembered the summers of 1816 and 1817 when his uncle Thomas Williamson (Sr.), a respected cashier of the Bank of Virginia in Norfolk, invited the extended family to spend a week at the Ferry with their children. He wrote that "on these occasions the Williamsons, McIntoshes, Walkes, Thoroughgoods and Moseleys, with other relations and friends, would make up an excursion or fishing parties to the Lynnhaven Bay. The fisherman and servants were sent in advance with tents, furniture and refreshments for the company." He remembered how "the children and nurses rambled along the bay shore, looking for sea-shells and enjoying the sea breeze, while the ladies and gentlemen were dancing or listening to the music." Nostalgically, he wrote about the trip back to Ferry at the end of the day: "As we rowed along, we little thought that the pleasant scenes of our childhood would soon be deserted by those we had known and loved so long."

Thomas Williamson died on March 31, 1888.

A Williamson family member fondly remembered a visit with her cousin, a descendant of Thomas Williamson (Jr.), in June 1914:

> *I have just come back from a visit to Cousin Thom Williamson who is a retired Admiral in the U.S.N.…It was just like a Williamson to ask a cousin whom they did not know to share their hospitality and have a good time.…The household reminded me of what I had heard of the joyous milieu of Great-grandfather Thom Williamson. The Admiral plays charming dance music for his grand-daughters and their midshipmen friends and spends his leisure in domestic pleasures and duties.*

Even though the manor house no longer stands, the spirit of Thomas Williamson still seems to come visit his old homestead. While he never lived at the house that stands today, he would have surely come to visit his first cousin, Charles McIntosh, who owned the then newly built Ferry Plantation House. One of the first recorded experiences with him happened with one of Belinda's grandchildren when they were very young. Belinda described the experience in her book *Ghosts, Witches & Weird Tales of Virginia Beach.* They were at Ferry one day, and as they were heading up the stairs to the second floor, her grandchild stopped at the turn of the stairs, pointed and said someone was up there. Belinda made assurances that no one was there, and they proceeded up the stairs. The child again insisted that someone was there. Belinda explained that they were probably seeing the shadows from the trees that were blowing in the wind and that they were there all alone. They continued with their day, but when it came time to leave, Belinda's grandchild looked up to the top of those same stairs and said, "The man with the dirty shirt is back." Belinda gathered her things, and they quickly left the house.

Several months later, they were at the house again. Belinda was busy painting when a storm came up. They decided to pack up and leave when

Second-story landing where the spirit of an artist, Thomas H. Williamson, is frequently seen. *Author's collection.*

the rain let up, and as she was gathering up her tools, her grandchild asked, "Nanny, what is he painting?" Belinda explained that she was just packing up the painting tools, but the child said, "He is painting, Nanny, and his shirt is dirty." Belinda thought that maybe they were referring to the man who had done the plastering. To a child, his shirt would look dirty with the plaster on it. But the child was sure that this was a different man.

Thomas Hoomes Williamson. *Courtesy of the Stafford Museum.*

A few weeks later, Belinda's grandchild was drawing in the upstairs Green Room, which is right off the second-story landing, and asked Belinda for some paints. She explained that she didn't have any in the house. Her grandchild, facing away from the landing, turned around and stared into the hallway, saying, "He is painting a picture, the man with the dirty shirt. Could I have some of his paints?" Belinda hurried to the door, but there was no one in the hall. On another occasion, Belinda asked the young child to describe the man to a visitor. He was described as "an old man with a dirty shirt and a beard, he was painting and he didn't have any feet." The visitor told Belinda to take this seriously because the child had seen something. He shared that most apparitions don't have feet.

The spirit seen on the landing seems to be that of Thomas Williamson. We know he was a painter, and the landing at the top of the second-floor stairs is very bright due to floor-length windows that used to lead to the porches on both sides. This would be the perfect location to paint. As an artist, his shirt would seem "dirty" to a child. It is also interesting to note that at times, small children will refuse to go up those second-story steps. They stop at the bottom and will not go any farther. Due to this, one of our volunteers, Gerry, will always go up those steps first if she has small children on the tour so she can block the view of any spirits possibly standing at the top. Volunteers sometimes bring their dogs to the house, and there are times they also refuse to go upstairs. Gerry said that she and Belinda used to bring their dogs all the time. Most days they were fine, and the dogs would run all over the house. Other days, the dogs would get to the bottom of those steps, yelp and run away.

We have another validation that this presence is likely Thomas Williamson. In 2022, we invited medium Ambrosia Matthews to go through the house with us so we could learn about what and who she saw. She had first come to the house for a history tour. When she did, she said there was a tall man with a beard who kept getting right up in her face and saying, "You can see me? You can really see me?" She didn't want to let anyone else on the tour know this was happening, so she just had to motion for him to step back. When she returned to go through the house again, she told me that she picked up on a "painter" and described how he got right in her face. She asked me if he was a touchy-feely kind of man. I told her I really didn't have a way of knowing that. She said she very much got that impression of him—that he didn't tend to respect personal space. It is interesting that I later found notes from another medium who had visited the house in December 2005. He said that there was a "heroic male figure connected to the Civil War, very handsome, loved women, a touchy-feely presence." That same day in 2022, as we were finishing up, Ambrosia went into our upstairs bathroom but immediately came out. I asked her what was wrong, and she said, "The painter is in there." Ironically, this bathroom is right off the second-story landing at the top of the stairs.

While most of our stories take place within the house, we do have a few accounts from outside. There have been several experiences reported at the hanging tree, the old sycamore located a few hundred feet behind the house. Investigators and guests have witnessed orbs around the tree, but orbs are often dismissed with a natural explanation like dust or bugs. One psychic medium recorded hearing the wailing of women who were gathered under the magnolia tree but looking toward the hanging tree. An early volunteer told me that neighbors used to hear cries and weeping around the tree and would call the police, only to find no one there. One sensitive guest once told me that the spirit of a little girl (perhaps Bessie?) likes to play around both the magnolia and sycamore trees.

The courthouse is the oldest section of the Ferry Plantation House, and it seems to still hold on to the lives of those who frequently inhabited or made use of the space. They make their appearances, move items or sometimes only appear to the very young or four-legged! Some we can identify, like Henry and Thomas Williamson, but others remain a mystery as to who they were in life, like our Gliding Lady. Whether she is a Walke relative from the Manor House or someone attached to the land, she, like the others, seems to consider Ferry Plantation their home, and we're grateful that they are willing to share their beloved house with us.

THE McINTOSH HOME

Any place that's been loved is forever haunted by those that loved it.
—*Culley Holderfield,* Hemlock Hollow

THE McINTOSH FAMILY

GEORGE AND ELIZABETH McINTOSH

After the Walke Manor House burned down in 1828, the plantation changed hands several times in quick succession. In 1829, Thomas Williamson Sr. and his wife, Anne, sold it to George Newton, who quickly sold it back into the Walke family. Elizabeth Walke McIntosh was Anne Williamson's older sister, and the girls had grown up in the manor house. By 1830, Elizabeth and her husband, George McIntosh, had become the plantation's new owners.

George McIntosh and Thomas Williamson seemingly had a good but competitive relationship as brothers-in-law. In 1812, George bet Thomas that when Thomas Jefferson was in London recently, he personally met the king. The bet was not put to rest until Thomas Williamson wrote a letter to Jefferson himself! Jefferson responded, confirming that he had indeed met King George III, the queen and other members of the royal family.

In fact, it may not have been too unusual to receive a letter from Thomas Jefferson, as the Walkes were distant relatives. Jane Bolling Randolph united the two families by marrying into the Walke family through Anthony II in

George McIntosh. *Courtesy of the Virginia Museum of History & Culture (2002.159.1.UU).*

1750. We also have correspondence between George McIntosh and Jefferson early in 1812 regarding a shipment of gooseberry bushes that were shipped to George from his native Scotland. He was to pass them on to Jefferson, and the letters discuss the arrival of the plants and the delivery arrangement to Jefferson at Monticello.

George McIntosh was a wealthy merchant who immigrated to Virginia from Edinburgh, Scotland, in the late 1780s. He bought Summerville Plantation, which sat directly across the Thurston Branch of the Lynnhaven River from the Ferry. Rear Admiral Henry Walke described Summerville in *Brief Records and Recollections*: "It was built square, of brick covered with white stucco; was flat roofed and ornamented with black urns on the corners of the house and porches, and with the surrounding tall poplar trees and handsome arbor built on the bank of the river in front." Summerville stood where Steinhilber's Restaurant is now located in the Thalia area of Virginia Beach. Early records indicate that there was once a "McIntosh Bridge" that connected Thalia to the peninsula where Ferry Plantation is located.

Legend says that George McIntosh would stand out on his balcony at Summerville and gaze lovingly across the river to the young Elizabeth Mason Walke as she stood on the porch of her family's manor house. The couple married at the Ferry on May 28, 1801. By this time, George had already proven himself in the Norfolk community through his successful mercantile business. In addition to now owning Ferry Plantation, he also purchased a second stately home in downtown Norfolk.

Sadly, the first year of marriage was one of hardship for the young McIntosh couple. George spent most of 1802 trying to prove the innocence of a slave named Jeremiah Cornick, who was falsely accused of planning a slave revolt in Norfolk on Easter of that same year. George spent endless hours gathering witness testimony and sent letters to then Governor James Monroe presenting evidence of his innocence. However, Jeremiah was still found guilty. In the midst of a contentious political time, Norfolk Mayor John

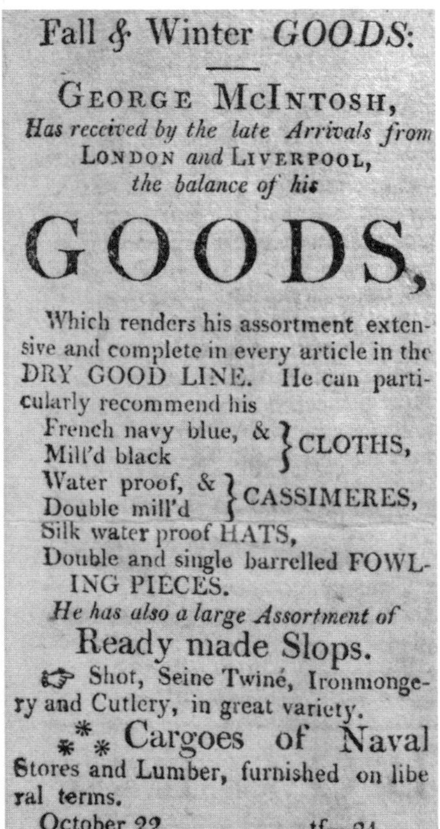

Fall & Winter *GOODS*:

GEORGE McINTOSH,
Has received by the late Arrivals from
LONDON *and* LIVERPOOL,
the balance of his

GOODS,

Which renders his assortment extensive and complete in every article in the DRY GOOD LINE. He can particularly recommend his
French navy blue, & Mill'd black } CLOTHS,
Water proof, & Double mill'd } CASSIMERES,
Silk water proof HATS,
Double and single barrelled FOWLING PIECES.
He has also a large Assortment of
Ready made Slops.
☞ Shot, Seine Twine, Ironmongery and Cutlery, in great variety.
⁂ Cargoes of Naval Stores and Lumber, furnished on liberal terms.
October 22. tf—24

Above: Summerville Plantation, home of George McIntosh. *Courtesy of the Friends of Ferry Plantation House.*

Left: An 1802 newspaper ad for George McIntosh's dry goods store in Norfolk, Virginia. *Courtesy of the Friends of Ferry Plantation House.*

View of the original Ferry Plantation land across the river from George McIntosh's Summerville Plantation. Steinhilber's Restaurant now stands on this location. *Author's collection.*

Cowper (also the Norfolk city judge) needed someone to make an example of to quiet the fears and rumors of a slave uprising that were running rampant throughout Norfolk and the surrounding areas. Ferry Plantation has a copy of the handwritten letter that Jeremiah wrote to George McIntosh on May 27, 1802, the day before his execution:

> *I have only to employ my time in the most earnest manner in endeavouring to make peace with my God who I call this day to witness my innocence. Perhaps I may never see you more. Therefore Gratitude binds me to return to you my most sincere thanks for the many favours received at your hands. Pray Sir take care of my wife and the dear little ones, and I hope that you and yours may be happy hear* [sic] *and hereafter. It is the sincere wish of the innocent but unfortunate Jeremiah.*

This speaks highly of the character of George McIntosh. He put his business and family's reputation on the line to speak out for what was right. This was a time when speaking out could have cost him his livelihood and possibly his life. However, he believed in Jeremiah's innocence until the day he died. He made this clear in an interview in his last years of life. It is also clear that George McIntosh had a strong sense of justice and integrity and successfully passed down these values to his children.

CAPTAIN CHARLES FLEMING McINTOSH

When George and Elizabeth McIntosh took ownership of Ferry Plantation, they salvaged as many bricks as they could save from the burned manor house. In 1830, they added the recovered bricks to the old courthouse, now being used as an outdoor kitchen, and built the middle section of the current Ferry Plantation House. One of their five children, Charles Fleming McIntosh, born on October 24, 1812, was just graduating from West Point with his naval commission at the age of seventeen. He lived as a bachelor at the Ferry for nearly twenty years before marrying Isabella Donaldson Thorburn, the daughter of his father's business partner, on December 4, 1849.

Over the next twelve years, Charles and Isabella had six children: George, Anne "Nannie," Isabella "Belle," Helen Winder, Elizabeth "Bessie" and Charles Jr. During this time, it was not uncommon for children to die young, and Helen and Charles Jr. died as babies. A few years later, on December 12, 1865, little Bessie passed away the day after her fifth birthday.

At the time that Charles was living at Ferry Plantation, he was working for the U.S. Navy at Gosport Naval Yard (later to become the Norfolk Naval Shipyard). When Virginia seceded from the Union in 1861, Charles resigned. He didn't agree with the secession and didn't want to serve under the Confederacy since Gosport now fell under the Southern command. However, against his wishes, he was drafted back into military service at the start of the Civil War to fight for the Confederate States Navy. In March 1862, he received orders to report to Louisiana. Charles would be leaving behind Isabella and their children at Ferry Plantation. When he left, Isabella was pregnant with their sixth child. George was eleven years old, Nannie was seven, Belle was five and Bessie was two. Little Helen had died three years earlier. Isabella would now not only be raising the children on her own but would also have new responsibilities in the running and management of the plantation.

Charles was ordered to Louisiana, where he was to command the CSS *Louisiana*, one of the newest ironclad ships. His role would be to defend the Confederacy by protecting New Orleans from being taken over by Union troops, who were making their way up the Mississippi River toward the city. When Charles arrived in Louisiana, he found that the construction of the *Louisiana* was not close to being completed. He and his soldiers worked day and night alongside the construction workers, trying to get the ship ready for the impending battle.

Top: Captain Charles Fleming McIntosh, CSN. *Courtesy of Sargeant Memorial Collection, Norfolk Public Library.*

Bottom: David G. Farragut Memorial, Washington, D.C. *Author's collection.*

Finally, the call came to send the *Louisiana* to Fort St. Philip and Fort Jackson on April 20, 1862. These Confederate forts were located south of New Orleans and were on opposite sides of the Mississippi River. They were to be used to block the Northern passage of the Union navy up the Mississippi. The *Louisiana* was still not ready, so it had to be towed and then moored to the shore beside Fort St. Philip, in the hopes that construction would continue. Only six of the ironclad's sixteen cannons were functional due to a design flaw and the fact that being moored to the riverbank prevented the use of the remaining guns.

The Union fleet was under the command of Flag Officer David G. Farragut. The irony and tragedy of this event is that Charles and Farragut knew each other and had served together in prior military assignments. Charles had served under Farragut on the USS *Saratoga* during the Mexican-American War. Now they were on opposing sides of the war and preparing to fight each other.

During the early hours of April 24, the USS *Cayuga* ran through the blockade between the two Confederate forts, and the battle began. Through the smoke, darkness and confusion, it's difficult to know the exact chronology of events. At one point during the battle, the USS *Iroquois* got caught in the strong river current and bumped into the CSS *Louisiana*. Charles was not able to fire due to a design flaw of the portholes being oval instead of circular. Fearing that the Union soldiers would board his ship, he ordered all his men on the upper deck. Joseph B. Wilkinson Jr. was on the *Louisiana* and remembers the event through a letter that was later published by

Cowardin & Hammersley in the *Daily Dispatch* in Richmond, Virginia, on May 21, 1862:

> *I arrived on board the Louisiana on the morning of the 23rd of April. Throughout the day Captain McIntosh manifested the greatest energy in spurring the workmen on, remaining on deck the whole time, and passing a sleepless night, in his haste and zeal to prepare the boat for the coming combat. During the action on the morning of the 24th he stood calmly on deck giving his orders amid a shower of grape and storm of shells, till struck by three grapeshot—one in each arm and his leg. He still kept the deck, through lying down, and exclaiming, smiling, "Such is the fate of war," and he did not complain. All that was in his power was done for the safety of New Orleans, and all of his officers and men were unanimous in their praises of his valor.*

The battle only lasted two and a half hours and was over by daybreak. It was a decisive win for the Union. Farragut continued to New Orleans, took over the city and raised the U.S. flag. The wounded soldiers from the battle were moved to New Orleans, but Charles refused to go until all his men were moved first. He didn't arrive in the city until May 1, nearly a week after he sustained life-threatening injuries in the battle. On May 4, 1862, the *Sunday Delta* in New Orleans wrote:

> *The gallant Capt. McIntosh, who was so dreadfully wounded in the fight of the gunboats, now lies in very critical condition in the Charity Hospital in this City. Capt. McIntosh occupied the most prominent and exposed position on the outer deck of the Louisiana, and when he was struck, the*

Farragut's Fleet Passing the Forts Below New Orleans, painted between 1863 and 1867 by Mauritz Frederick de Haas. *Courtesy of the Historic New Orleans Collection.*

> *ship which the Louisiana was fighting nearly touched her side. He was thrown by the force of the concussion a distance of forty or fifty feet. Both his arms were badly fractured; one has been amputated, and his knee pan was cut off. Despite these terrible wounds the gallant officer bears himself with great fortitude and excellent spirits.*

Miraculously, Charles lived with his mortal wounds for nineteen days. On the night of May 13, 1862, at six o'clock, he succumbed to his injuries. His funeral was held on May 14 at five o'clock at the Fourth Presbyterian Church in New Orleans. The *Daily Picayune* published an article on May 15, 1862, stating:

> *Another of the brave and devoted officers of the gunboat fleet who fell, mortally wounded, in the ineffectual effort to defend the river approach to the City, was buried yesterday, a large number of his fellow officers, citizens, and others, of both sexes, attending the obsequies.*

Since he was far from home, Charles was buried at the Girod Cemetery in New Orleans. It was always assumed that Charles was later moved to the Cedar Grove Cemetery in Norfolk, Virginia, because there is a tombstone for him there in the McIntosh family plot. However, the McIntosh family was contacted in the 1950s, saying that they had found Charles's tomb

McIntosh family burial plot at Cedar Grove Cemetery in Norfolk, Virginia. *Author's collection.*

and wanted to know if the family wanted him moved. The grounds of the cemetery were soon to be developed into a shopping center and a sports arena. In speaking with a McIntosh descendant, I learned that the family worried that if they moved his body to Norfolk, there would already be a body mistakenly buried in his plot. So, the family decided to leave him where he was. Sadly, his body, along with any others that were unclaimed, now lies under the Mercedes-Benz Superdome in New Orleans.

Charles passed away at age forty-nine, but he had a full life. Coming from an immigrant Scottish family on his father's side, he took his U.S. military service seriously and pledged loyalty to his country. He served his entire adult life, having given his time and effort to the fullest. The comments about his integrity, gallantry, fortitude, patriotism and excellent spirit portray the kind of man he was. These characteristics did not seem to change whether he was preparing the ship, fighting a battle or lay dying in a hospital bed. There is no doubt that Isabella and his children at Ferry Plantation were proud of his commitment and his ultimate sacrifice for their country. He was most surely missed by family and friends when he never returned to his beloved home along the banks of the Lynnhaven River.

ISABELLA THORBURN McINTOSH

Isabella Donaldson Thorburn was born on June 28, 1827, and married Charles McIntosh when she was twenty-two years old. Sadly, she was widowed at age thirty-five with four children and one more on the way. It's difficult to imagine what life would have been like while she anxiously waited and prayed that her husband would return home from war. She had the sole responsibility of running the plantation, raising her children and doing this with only sporadic news from the battlefront. We do, however, have some insights into her life during this harrowing time. Camilla Frances Loyall kept a diary from her home in Norfolk, Virginia, during the time that Charles was off fighting in Louisiana. She provides us snippets of information and perspective on how families in Norfolk handled their soldiers fighting near New Orleans. Loyall found herself in an uncomfortable situation, as David Farragut was her brother-in-law and well known to the families in Norfolk. Many local men besides Charles McIntosh had previously served with Farragut. On May 1, 1862, she wrote this about Isabella McIntosh: "Mrs. McIntosh is also miserable about her husband who is reported wounded." On May 2, she wrote, "Mrs. McIntosh also received a telegram today from Captain Whittle saying that her husband had his arm shot off." On May 7, she records that they received word that Charles was badly wounded and his right arm was amputated. On May 31, 1862, she wrote this heart-wrenching account:

> *In the afternoon, I heard of Capt. McIntosh's death. The news came through a letter from Capt. Dornin to John McIntosh* [Charles's brother]. *Mrs. Mc fainted when the news reached her. Poor woman, how I sympathize with her. She was so hopeful that his life would be spared.*

Isabella was eight months pregnant when she received this news. In her book *Love & Duty: Confederate Widows and the Emotional Politics of Loss*, Angela Esco Elder explained that the first son born after the death of a Civil War soldier was traditionally named after his deceased father. This was the case with Isabella's baby boy, whom she named Charles Fleming McIntosh. To add more grief to her already broken heart, Isabella's little boy died one month after his first birthday. Three months earlier, George McIntosh Sr. passed away at the age of ninety-five. Rear Admiral Henry Walke wrote in *Brief Recollections and Records* that George remained loyal to the U.S. government and the Union during the Civil War. Walke continued, "His property was confiscated by the Confederates, which with the loss of his son, Captain McIntosh, C.S.N., preyed on his mind, and no doubt (as he was advanced in years) hastened his death." Unfortunately, Isabella's losses wouldn't end there. Three years later, her youngest daughter, Bessie, passed away from diphtheria at the age of five.

Isabella Donaldson Thorburn McIntosh. *Courtesy of the Virginia Museum of History & Culture (2002.159.1.MM).*

Isabella McIntosh would live to be eighty-two years old, surviving her husband and all but one of her six children. On April 24, 1871, court records indicate that she was ordered to sell Ferry Plantation and their property in Norfolk to help pay off debts. We also see through the *Landmark News* article from January 31, 1891, "Old Colonial Mansion Falls Before the Tide of Progress," that Charles's brother, John Elphinstone McIntosh, stated in his will that Isabella could live in the Norfolk family home on Granby Street for the remainder of her life. It's endearing to learn that John made sure that his brother's widow was taken care of. She lived there until her death on November 26, 1909. The article continues to state that the home was then sold and torn down by developers in favor of a more modern structure.

FERRY PLANTATION HOUSE DURING THE CIVIL WAR

During the Civil War, Ferry Plantation became a safe house for Walke family members whose homes were either burned or confiscated by both Union and Confederate troops in Norfolk. Many cousins left the city to come live with Isabella McIntosh during this time. While the men were off fighting, the women were busy at Ferry. In addition to keeping the plantation up and running, the salt bog that was used by the Walkes since the 1700s became crucial during the war. Large pans of salt water were boiled over open fires, producing five bushels of salt per day. This practice continued until the Union troops destroyed the saltworks during the war, and it was never rebuilt. The women also raised acres of onions. When onions were mashed and pulverized, they were made into a poultice and put on open wounds to stop infection. The Ferry women sent hundreds of pounds of onions into the war zones to be used for the purpose of treating

Ferry Farm Plantation by William George "Rip" Rylance. *Courtesy of the Friends of Ferry Plantation House.*

the injured soldiers. They also collected the nitre from the charcoal in the smokehouse that was used in the making of black powder. They grew blackberries (which are still on Ferry property) to help combat diarrhea, and the roots were used as an astringent. In addition, they wove and rolled yards of bandages that they made out of flax and cotton. All of these items were sent to the battlefields to help the soldiers, many of whom were their husbands, sons, brothers and neighbors.

CIVIL WAR-ERA SPIRITS OF FERRY PLANTATION HOUSE

SPIRIT OF BESSIE

One of the best-known and loved spirits of Ferry Plantation House is that of little Bessie McIntosh. Bessie died on December 12, 1865, the day after her fifth birthday. She makes herself known in a variety of ways. Some people will feel a wisp of air blow past them, as if a child has just run by. Others, myself included, will feel tugs on their shirts or skirts, as if a child is trying to get their attention. I also heard a child talking one day in the Green Room as I was working nearby. Perhaps the most common claim I hear from guests is that while they are in the Best Parlor, they will feel Bessie grab a few fingers, like little children do, and she will swing their arm back and forth. Cody claims that she does this with him when he's giving tours. One guest, who was a sensitive, told me that Bessie often comes along with me on my tours. She said she seems a bit bored as we go through the rooms, but she wants to be with everyone. In his interview with 13 News Now on October 25, 2022, Cody said of Bessie, "She's actually my hug when I come into the house every day. When I come in, I say 'Hi, House!' and I get a hug right around my thighs."

Ann Henley was once giving a tour to a young couple, and she was explaining the use of a "pee pot." She said the man suddenly got a shocked look on his face. She was afraid she had offended him by calling it a "pee pot" instead of a chamber pot. He waited until she was done and then told her that while she was talking, he felt two arms reach up and wrap around his waist. He said it had to have been a child. Ann said she would've had to have used that "pee pot" if that had happened to her!

In their book *Ghosts, Witches & Weird Tales of Virginia Beach*, Lillie Gilbert, Belinda Nash and Deni Norred-Williams describe a time when some teens came into the house when it was abandoned back in the 1980s. One saw a little girl run up the stairs and vanish. The not-so-brave group ran out and never came back. This story was told to Belinda by the mother of one of the teens who said her daughter came home "white as a ghost." The authors tell of another experience that happened in July 2003. While the event is recorded in their book, Belinda Nash gave more details in the records at Ferry. At the time that she wrote this, they didn't have a name for the little girl but knew she was there in the house. They kept sensing the name "Elizabeth," which is chilling because that is Bessie's given name. Belinda wrote:

> *The first time that she was sighted and recorded was on July 10, 2003. The Trial of Grace Sherwood was taking place that day. Lots of activity outside and inside the house. A clergyman was here as part of our re-enactment. After we finished, we all came into the house to eat and change out of costume. As Tony walked into the dining room he was met by the unexpected, a little girl aged six to eight. She appeared out of nowhere. She made her way past him, took a few steps and turned, looked over her shoulder and stared at him. She had a sad look on her face and seemed to be looking for something or someone. She then vanished through the landside wall. Tony could describe her as wearing a pale blue dress, not much color, her hair was dark and in ringlets. She had no fancy trappings on her dress but it was of good quality. Others have seen this little girl as well. When the house was boarded up for twelve years, adventure seekers would make their way into the house only to be frightened off by the little girl playing on the back stairs. Could this be our little Elizabeth?*

In 2020, the website Try to Scare Me published the story of when one of the Ferry volunteers had a friend come by one day when the house wasn't open for tours. While showing her around the grounds, her friend became anxious and wanted to leave. Once they got down to the parking lot, the friend said she saw a little girl with ringlets and Mary Jane shoes standing in front of the outside brick oven. I had a guest once tell me that Bessie likes to play around the magnolia tree that stands very close to this spot.

These descriptions given by the clergyman and the volunteer's friend perfectly match the only picture we have of Bessie McIntosh. Her dark hair is in ringlets, and she wears a light-colored dress with Mary Jane–type shoes. This picture, however, was not found at the then Virginia Historical Society until after these events so these guests would not have seen her picture

Left: Elizabeth "Bessie" Walke McIntosh. *Courtesy of the Virginia Museum of History & Culture (2002.159.1.SS).*

Opposite: Grave of Elizabeth "Bessie" Walke McIntosh at Cedar Grove Cemetery in Norfolk, Virginia. Bessie died the day after her fifth birthday. *Author's collection.*

beforehand. It's interesting, and a little sad, that when the paranormal investigators at the house ask Bessie how old she is, she will say four because she died before her family could celebrate her fifth birthday.

I personally have had one other experience with Bessie. I had just finished a tour, and several of the guests and I were sitting in the conference room talking. Ironically, two of these guests were sensitives and could see our spirits. While we were talking, they both said that Bessie had come into the room but immediately went and stood behind my chair. They explained that she was peeking around as if shy. They told me they could tell she was comfortable with me, so stayed right behind me, like a little child does. Even though I can't see our spirits, I do talk to them because I know they are there. Last December, I happened to be at the house on Bessie's birthday, and as I was walking down the stairs to leave, I told Bessie I hoped she would have a good birthday. Right then, I heard a little child's voice come from the floor above.

SPIRIT OF CAPTAIN CHARLES FLEMING McINTOSH

You often hear people say that when someone dies, their spirit returns to the place where they were happiest. This seems to be the case with Charles

McIntosh, the captain who died during the Battle of New Orleans in 1862. Ferry Plantation was his home when he was fatally wounded. As with any soldier heading off to battle, I'm sure he hoped to return but knew that there was a chance he wouldn't. However, it seems like Charles did make his way home after his death in Louisiana.

While maybe not one of our more prevalent ghosts, Charles is known to make an occasional appearance. Cody shared that Charles would often hit one particular volunteer on the shoulder with his cane. It is generally said in the house that if you smell cigar smoke, Charles is near. A medium once told me that in the parlor she saw a man wearing a vest with a pocket watch on a chain. She described him as very observant and standing with his hand in his front vest pocket. Even though she didn't smell anything, she saw him smoking. This same medium, who didn't know the home's history, picked up the name "Charles." I asked which one, since we had two men named Charles who lived in the house. She said the last name has an "s." I asked if it was McIntosh or Barnett, and she paused as if she was listening and then said McIntosh. Through the years, mediums have claimed that Charles keeps a close watch over the house. They say he is glad that the house has been restored; however, he continues to be watchful as he doesn't want to see the house destroyed.

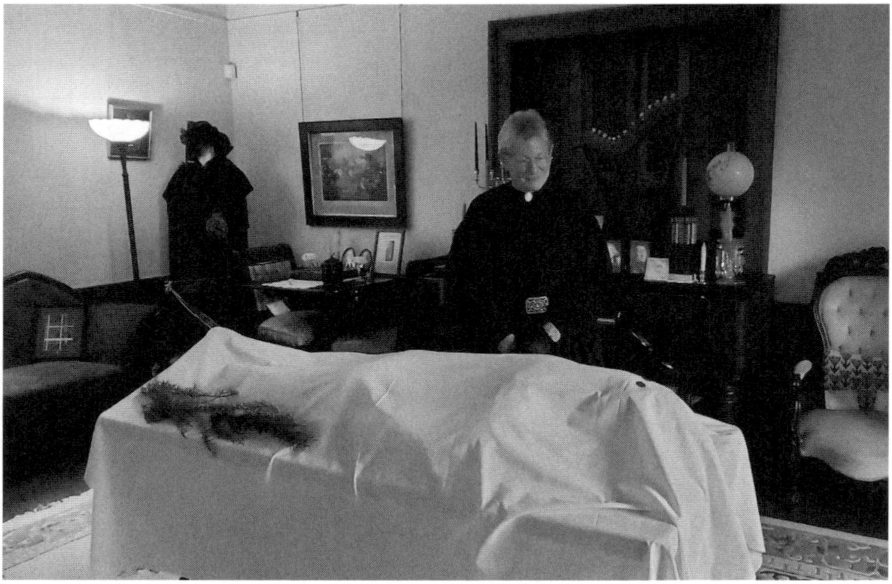

Volunteer Ann Henley standing over the mock body in the Best Parlor, demonstrating traditional mourning practices. *Author's collection.*

Every October, the volunteers at Ferry Plantation put the house in mourning. We lay out a mannequin in the Best Parlor, cover it with a sheet, place coins on the eyes and put herbs around the body. This was the common mourning ritual during the Victorian period. Before there were funeral parlors, families would lay out their dead in the parlor of their home. The body would remain for a few days to see if they would "wake" up, thus giving us the modern term *wake* for the time before a person is buried. The medium who picked up on Charles's name was visiting the house during this time of mourning. When we were in the parlor, I was explaining the various mourning practices, and she said that Charles told her that we had the wrong coins on the eyes of our "deceased relative." We had placed two modern-day quarters over the eyes, as we didn't have any nineteenth-century coins readily available.

In his book *Encounters with the Paranormal*, Mike Ricksecker wrote about an experience he had in the Best Parlor. He was also there when the house was in mourning, and when he walked into the parlor, he had a physical reaction with chills and a tingling, static-like feeling. He asked the spirits what they thought of our mock funerary scene. He immediately got the feeling that they didn't like it. The room got cold. He felt it was a woman letting him know to tell the caretakers of Ferry to take it down. She affirmed that, yes, wakes were held in that room, but it wasn't the focal point. She said many good times were had there as well. Typically, the parlor would have been the room for entertaining guests with music, dancing, socializing and playing games. In fact, once funeral parlors were opened and wakes were no longer held in private homes, the parlor became known as the living room.

SPIRIT OF ISABELLA THORBURN McINTOSH

Isabella McIntosh, Charles's wife and Bessie's mother, suffered tremendous loss through the deaths of her husband, three children and father-in-law within a very short period of time. There have been reports of a female spirit at Ferry that seems to be grieving. Some claim to have seen this woman in a rocking chair looking out of one of the second-story windows. Some feel she is looking out, waiting for her husband to return home. When medium Ambrosia Matthews first visited the house, she was walking by a nineteenth-century mourning dress with a hoop skirt when she heard a spirit tell her how uncomfortable those dresses were to wear. Could this have been Isabella McIntosh, who would've been in a constant state of mourning for many years?

Sherry Baier is a clairaudient and clairsentient, meaning that she can talk to and feel spirits. While visiting Ferry Plantation in 2013 with 7 Cities Paranormal, Sherry "sensed a nice woman with good energy sitting near the window in the courthouse, rocking in her chair. She would push her chair with just her right foot. This was her favorite room. She would sit there and wait for her traveling husband to come home. She had four children. Two were sons, one son passed early, the other became a very influential businessman." Could this also be Isabella, waiting for Charles to return from his military duties?

One of the best paranormal photos we have from Ferry is believed to be that of Isabella. It was taken in the reflection of the landside window in the Best Parlor. You can clearly see a woman, looking down. She has brown hair, pulled back from her face. She wears a patterned blue dress with a white collar. Her dress bumps out over her stomach, clearly showing that she is pregnant. Isabella was pregnant with their sixth child when she would have stood by that very window, waiting for her husband, Charles, to return from war. Sadly, he never returned.

On the other hand, Isabella has also been described as being very bubbly, flirtatious and loving to dance. I believe she can be both. She was a person just like anyone else. She suffered more loss than she should have, but that doesn't mean that she didn't have the outgoing, friendly personality of someone who liked to entertain. Some paranormal investigators, as well as Ferry volunteers, have awakened in the middle of the night to hear a full-blown dinner party happening downstairs—glasses clinking, people laughing and music playing. I have no doubts that the McIntoshes would have hosted parties just like this. Apparently, they continue to do so nearly two hundred years later.

Cody has brought up an interesting point about the ghost of Isabella. The picture that was captured in the window would be an example of a residual haunting. This means that the energy was imprinted on the environment (in this case the Best Parlor), and a scene from the past will play over and over again. For instance, if someone walked out their front door every morning at 8:00 a.m., when that person dies, their spirit may still be seen walking out the door at that same time every day. Or sometimes, residual sightings will happen on an anniversary, like every spring or every year on a specific date. Residual spirits do not acknowledge the presence of the living. They go about their lives like they did all those years ago. On the other hand, an intelligent haunting means that the spirit is aware of the living and will sometimes interact with us. This is where we hear about ghosts answering specific questions or knocking or making other noises on command. We know they understand and see us through the "intelligent" responses they give. In the case of Isabella, we have both a residual and an intelligent spirit. She residually waits by the window for her husband to return from war, but she also interacts with living people in the house. This is unusual, as spirits are normally one or the other but generally not both.

I find comfort in the fact that Charles, Isabella and Bessie still remain in the house together. The other three children grew to be adults and had families of their own, but it seems that Bessie and her parents decided to return and make their forever home at Ferry Plantation House.

SPIRIT OF SALLY REBECCA WALKE

When Sherry Baier visited the house, she said that she felt that most of the ladies who lived at Ferry Plantation were very happy there. One particular cousin who came to live at the McIntosh house during the Civil War was Sally Rebecca Walke. Born on October 27, 1842, she is said to have come with her father because their home in Norfolk had been burned by Union troops. Many of the Walke family came to Ferry during the war because it was out in the country in a safe area. The story is told that Sally, formally named Sarah, had a fiancé named John who was off fighting in the war. It wasn't long after she had moved to Ferry that Sally received word that her beloved was killed in battle. On April 6, 1863, a grieving Sally planted a magnolia tree outside her window at Ferry in remembrance of him. That magnolia tree still stands today.

Even through her time of grief, Sally must have enjoyed her time at Ferry because she chose to come back to stay after her death in 1917. In their book *Ghosts, Witches & Weird Tales of Virginia Beach*, Belinda Nash, Lillie Gilbert and Deni Norred-Williams described Sally as a tall, dark-haired girl in her twenties, dressed in gray and black, who is often seen leaning against the mantel in the conference room. It is said that she kept a shrine to her fallen soldier on this mantel in what used to be her bedroom. This shrine included candles, a snippet of John's hair in a locket and a sword hung above the fireplace. The 1863 mantel has been replaced, but some visitors have come into the room to see Sally at the mantel, crying. They catch the faint glow of candles along with the scent of freshly mown hay.

The magnolia tree that Sally planted is right outside her bedroom window. Surely she must have gazed at that tree every morning, grieving

Second-floor view of the magnolia tree said to be planted by Sally Rebecca Walke in 1863. *Author's collection.*

and remembering her fallen fiancé. It's interesting to note that, over time, the roots of the magnolia had pulled the tree off center so it no longer lined up with the landside front door. However, nature has since stepped in and pulled it upright again. You can see the curve where the correction was made. Belinda claimed that Mother Nature was looking out after Sally Rebecca Walke. The magnolia is now registered as a Champion Tree of Virginia and a Notable Tree of Virginia Beach.

In her book, Belinda told the story about an encounter with Sally Rebecca. The house was hosting a Red Hat Society Fashion Show, and it was a very hot July day in 2004. Belinda was under six layers of colonial clothes but felt a cold chill go through her as she told a group of women the story of Sally Rebecca. Everyone in the room felt the chill. Belinda explained, "As it was told to me, if you are speaking about a departed one who is present in the room, that departed one will let you know of its presence."

It is interesting to note that a medium from the Edgar Cayce Foundation picked up the name Sally in the house in February 1997. Later that same year, a second medium visiting the house picked up the same name. Try to Scare Me claims that years later, a paranormal team was investigating Ferry, and they asked Sally, "Why do you stand at the fireplace?" A mournful woman's voice replied, "I'm so chilled."

One of my guests on a tour believes that she saw Sally. We were at the end of the tour, and I had taken the group outside to talk about the magnolia tree. I told Sally's story and how she would look out the window at the tree to remember her fiancé. All of a sudden, this girl said, "Oh! Okay, that makes sense now!" I asked what she was talking about, and she said that as she was walking up the sidewalk before the tour, she saw a woman with long hair looking out the window at her. Then she said when we stepped outside to the other side of the house, she saw the same girl again but looking out the back window from the same room. From the description I gave, she felt she had seen Sally, still looking out the window, remembering her lost love.

SPIRIT OF ERIC

One of our more active spirits in the house is that of a little boy named Eric. The interesting thing is that we have no historical record of him. We believe he was likely a cousin to the Walkes/McIntoshes, although we have found no records with his name. The background we have on him comes only from medium accounts and information obtained through paranormal investigations.

Eric is said to be around eight years old. We believe he is still at Ferry because it is said that he tragically fell to his death out of the landside window of our conference room in the mid- to late 1800s. Even today, some have sensed him pulling guests back away from that window. (We know that his fall would have been after 1850, when that addition to the house was added.) Despite his devastating story, Eric is very much our prankster and mischievous little spirit.

In Belinda's collaboration book *Ghosts, Witches & Weird Tales of Virginia Beach*, she revealed how a psychic visiting the house in the late 1990s heard the name Eric in association with the small boy seen at the house. She also told the story about a group of Old Dominion University students who were doing design work on Ferry in 1997. The house was empty at the time, so they had all put their lunches up on the mantel in the library. A Snickers bar was left at the end of the mantel. As the team worked and students were all in different areas of the room, the candy bar flew off the mantel and fell about four feet away. The students watched in awe. They tried to re-create it but couldn't get it to fall. When they pushed it, it fell straight to the floor, not four feet away. Belinda also described how this same group would put a ball in the house, and they would find it had moved from room to room. In his book *Haunted Virginia Beach*, Alpheus Chewning continued to explain that this group of ODU students had a hard time keeping track of their supplies while they were working in the house. Tools would be in different places from where they had left them the day before. One of the psychics who visited the house in 1997 said there is a little boy between the ages of seven and ten who runs through the house and likes to hide things. The Snickers, the ball and the moving tools have all been attributed to the playful spirit of Eric.

When Sherry Baier visited the house in 2013, she picked up on a mischievous little boy in the nursery. She claimed that when everyone was asleep, he'd sneak out of the house, get on his horse and ride off without anyone knowing. He got into trouble often. She said he would ride down to the river to see if any ships had brought back sweets from England. She felt that he also loved to prank the enslaved people. He would jump out from behind a tree to scare them. He supposedly loved horses, but it was dangerous around them because he was always jumping around. She said that he would ride "like a bat out of hell." She described him as about five feet tall, with dark hair and wearing a Peter Pan–type collared shirt and jacket. She said he hated it and felt like it was for babies; he wanted to dress like his father. She very much felt that this was the boy who fell out of the window to his death.

I have had other guests describe Eric to me as being blond. I once had a young girl on a tour who was clearly gifted in sensing our spirits, but it was very much a gift in progress. Anything she would see or hear, she would just blurt out. There was a lot of validity in the things she said, but it was very uncontrolled and a bit chaotic. When we were going upstairs, she told us to be careful not to step on the little boy sitting on the steps. Later in the tour, when we reached the conference room, she said the little boy on the stairs was Eric. Not having any historical reference to this child, I asked her if she knew how he was related to the family. She quickly and matter-of-factly said that he was a cousin. I asked how she knew, and she said he just told her because he was now sitting in the chair right next to me. When Ambrosia Matthews was on her first visit to the house, she said she was in the gift shop and clearly saw a little blond boy run right across the hall toward the window. She said it was very fast and so lifelike that she thought it was real. Gerry noticed her expression and asked her what she had seen. At first she downplayed it, but Gerry persisted so Ambrosia told her. Gerry told her the story about Eric falling out of the window. Ambrosia then said that it all made sense.

While Eric has been seen all over the house, he seems to prefer to hang out and play tricks in the gift shop, which used to be the older boys' room. One day, we were having a board meeting and were standing around talking in the gift shop. Our resident skeptic, Joshua Husak, was standing next to a shelf full of tins of loose tea. One suddenly fell off and landed directly at his feet. We all stared at him. He tried to explain that he had moved his feet, making the floor shift, which made the tin fall. We all still stared at him, knowing that this wasn't what happened at all. He tried to re-create it, but all the other tins, even those closest to the edge of the shelf, remained in place.

One year, a good family friend, Brandon Campbell, helped me in the gift shop on the days I had tours. On one occasion after a tour, a guest was in the gift shop picking up a few items. He paid and was walking toward the door when he turned to Brandon and said, "Nothing paranormal really happens here, does it?" And just then, one of the tins of tea fell off the shelf and landed right at his feet. Brandon looked at him, smiled and said, "Sometimes." Brandon said the guest grabbed his bag and hurried out of the room. During his time at the house, Brandon also heard footsteps in the nursery, which is directly above the gift shop. Another time, he saw the closet door open all by

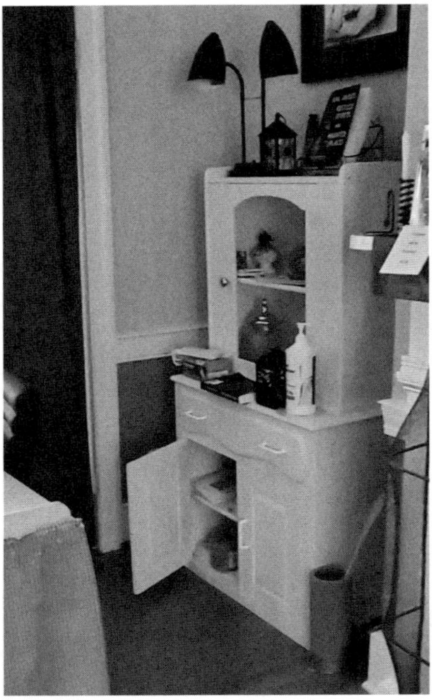

Cabinet door in the gift shop that frequently opens on its own. *Author's collection.*

itself. Most teenagers would have run out and never returned, but Brandon remained dedicated to his time at Ferry; he faithfully continued to help despite Eric's continued tricks.

The most common experience we've had in the gift shop since I've been with the house is that one of the cabinet doors opens on its own. I watched in amazement the first time I saw it on our security video. Then it continued to happen, over and over again. It is now such a common occurrence that we simply just close the cabinet door when we find it open and go about our business. It is possible to make the door open if you repeatedly pound on the top of the cabinet, but the times we've caught it opening, no one is nearby. In fact, it usually happens when no one is in the house at all. However, one time, it did open right as I walked into the room. I didn't find it open until later, but when I went back and looked at the video, it clearly opened just as I stepped into the room.

When Ambrosia Matthews visited the house, she said there was a mischievous little boy that liked to play tricks on people in the gift shop. We have some upper cabinets above the closets, and she said he likes to play in there. One day, when I was opening the house, one set of these cabinet doors was wide open. I asked her if Eric's the one who always opens the lower cabinet door. She paused, listened and then said that he just laughed, so it was likely him.

One afternoon while I was doing some research at the house, I was reading a book in our gift shop. I was sitting in a chair and kept feeling what felt like someone tapping the top of my head. I would brush my hand over my head and continue reading. Then it started again. I asked Eric if that was him, and while I didn't get a reply, I did move to the conference room and it didn't happen anymore. Paranormal investigators often interact with Eric when they come to the house because he is so active. They get responses on their equipment that they believe to be from him. Whether or not this is Eric, we do know he is the playful one in the house. And just like any child who tends to get into frequent trouble, he is often to blame at Ferry for cabinets left open and for pushing items off the shelves.

SPIRIT OF THE NANNY

Any late-night visitors to Ferry Plantation are all told not to go to the third-floor nursery after 10:00 p.m. We have the active spirit of a nanny that does not appreciate anyone coming up to the children's room late in the evening after she has gotten the little ones settled into bed for the night. In fact, she can get a little testy and tell people to "Get out!" She is very protective of the children in this space, as we believe she continues to watch over and take care of them. This third floor over the middle section of the house consists of a low-ceilinged nursery and a small bedroom for the nanny.

Ambrosia Matthews and other mediums who have seen the nanny describe her as a small-framed African American woman wearing all black. She is seen as serious, somber, no-nonsense and very unassuming. They say she is loving but strict. Other than asking people to leave, she doesn't often interact directly with those wishing to communicate with her. She gives the sense that she is there to do her job and doesn't like any attention focused on her. She also doesn't like outsiders being in her space.

We have picked up the name Angie for the nanny, but this hasn't been confirmed in any historical records, so we continue to refer to her simply as the nanny. On her bed, we have a picture of the Brander family who lived in Richmond. This picture includes their nanny, Julie. The family must have thought a lot of Julie to include her in the family portrait. Even though they were related to the Walkes, the Brander family never lived in Princess Anne County, so Julie was never the nanny at Ferry Plantation. However, Ambrosia said that our nanny looks very similar to Julie. She said that the nanny actually startled her because when she turned the corner to go up to the third floor, the nanny was standing right at the top of the steps in her black dress, staring down at her.

Legend has it that one day when the nanny was coming down the narrow flight of stairs, one of the children accidentally stepped on the back of her skirt, causing her to fall down the stairs, break her neck and die. Guests to Ferry who haven't felt anything anywhere else in the house will often feel weird on the third floor. I have seen visitors who didn't yet know the fate of the nanny come to the top of the steps, grab their neck and immediately go

Portrait of Elizabeth Louisa (Walke) Brander's family with their nanny, Julie, circa 1888.
Courtesy of the Friends of Ferry Plantation House.

back downstairs. One guest told me that she kept feeling like she was going to fall down the steps. Some people get a heavy sensation, while others feel comforted and safe. One phenomenon that I have experienced many times is to hear someone coming up the steps, only to look and see that no one is there. Only half of the staircase is carpeted, so the sound of feet hitting the wooden boards is very distinct.

In her book *Ghosts, Legends, and Lore of Hampton Roads*, Cecilia Petretto wrote that on the third floor, footsteps can be heard going back and forth, as if the nanny is walking a fussy baby or going between her room and the nursery to check on the children. She recorded that during a paranormal investigation, the nanny was asked, "How did you fall down the stairs?" The reply came in the form of a woman's voice saying, "Your children!"

When Ambrosia visited the house, she described the different spirits she felt and saw. With her permission, I recorded her on my phone as she went through the different rooms. As we were walking up the third-floor steps to the nursery, our volunteers George and Cindy Core heard a voice! Those of us closer to the top of the stairs didn't hear it until we played back my phone recording. It was a man's voice slowly whispering, "Why…is…she… here?" Certainly he was referring to Ambrosia, who could see the spirits who were not used to being seen. The interesting thing is that George was carrying a mini tape recorder flat in his hand where he couldn't accidentally hit any buttons. When they went to play back the tape, they realized that nothing had been recorded while they were on the steps, even though it was recording fine in the other areas of the house.

When we entered the nanny's room, Ambrosia asked her what her name was. She said the nanny ducked back into the room as if to say this wasn't about her, or as if it was improper for her to speak to Ambrosia. In the nursery, Ambrosia said she felt a little girl, around three years old, who kept taking her hand and pulling her like she wanted to show her something. Some say that the children run and hide when we come into the room. Others feel children all around. Some want to play, while others are sick in bed. Some say that the nanny waits by the door for us to leave. There is a general consensus among all who can sense the nanny that she doesn't want anyone in her room.

In June 2015, Full Moon Paranormal and 7 Cities Paranormal were doing an investigation at Ferry. When they reached the nanny's room, she promptly told them in an angry voice to "Get out!" But what they captured next is one of the most remarkable Electronic Voice Phenomena (EVP) that I have heard anywhere. When they asked, "Do you want us to get out?"

Footsteps are often heard on the stairs coming down from the nursery and nanny's room. *Author's collection.*

they captured what sounds like an older African American woman saying, "When I don't want nobody in my room, don't want nobody in my room!...I mean this *all* the way around." Her voice is very clear, and you can even hear the intonation of her voice. With permission from the team to share this, you are able to listen to this yourself, as it is posted under Full Moon Paranormal on YouTube as "The Ferry Plantation: Nanny EVP."

One night after an event, one of our volunteers decided to stay the night. She and two other volunteers decided to sleep in the nursery. They spread out their sleeping bags but only had about a foot in between each of them. When the volunteer lay down, she felt a tug on her sleeping bag. She asked if one of her friends was messing with her, and they assured her they weren't. She lay back down and again felt the tug. Instinctively, she unzipped the sleeping bag and opened it. When she did, she felt little arms wrap around her like a child was settling in with her. She said they stayed like that until she fell asleep. She was sure the little girl was Bessie.

In the book *Encounters with the Paranormal*, Shannon Heath shared her story from the same night. She was one of the other volunteers spending the night in the nursery. She described how once everyone was settled in, she had a hard time falling asleep because she was a little nervous and scared, this being her first time spending the night in the house. Suddenly, she felt someone move between her sleeping bag and that of her friend. She explained:

> *Then I felt a hand start to comb my hair. As freaky as this sounds, it really wasn't scary at all. This went on for a good five minutes when I realized it was one of the ghosts just trying to calm me down enough to fall asleep. At that point, I whispered, "I know you are trying to help, but this is making me more nervous. Can you stop please?" It stopped.*

One day, we were giving a tour to a talented group of mediums. They were visiting in October, when we had the house in mourning. One of the other traditions we practice is to cover all the mirrors with black veils, as families would have done when someone passed away. The fear was that the soul of the deceased person might get trapped in the mirror and not pass on to the next realm. Covering the mirrors prevented this from happening. A mirror hangs at the bottom of the stairs that lead to the third floor. As I was bringing the group up to the nursery, we found the black cloth that was covering that mirror in a heap on the floor. Cindy was helping me with the tour, and she had been the one to cover all of the mirrors that year. She explained that this was the only one that wouldn't stay up. You could see the

Third-floor nursery where the spirit of the nanny continues to keep watch over the children. *Author's collection.*

layers of extra tape she had used previously, trying to get it to stay in place. As she started to hang it up again, a girl in the back of the group said that it was the nanny who kept taking it down. I asked her what she meant. She said that the nanny said that she can't do her job when it's covered because she can't see who is coming up the steps. That made perfect sense because the nanny would have to be able to see who was coming up the stairs in order to protect the children. Cindy and I decided not to put it back up so we could respect her wishes. The girl in the back said, "She says thank you!"

I'm actually writing this next part from the nursery at Ferry Plantation. It's a bright, beautiful Saturday afternoon without a cloud in the sky. Even so, the nursery and nanny's room are always a little dark due to the smaller dormer windows on this third floor. The ceilings are considerably lower here, causing tall people on my tours to have to duck. The air conditioning flows out of small, circular vents on the ceiling, so guests often claim to feel a cold spot when in reality they find themselves standing under one of these vents. The nursery is fairly large, but not nearly large enough to house the more than fifteen children who were said to stay here during the Civil War. The small nanny's room is across the hall. In colonial times, the children were not allowed to have the run of the house. They were either in the nursery or outside. I have great admiration for the nanny, who never had time away from the children.

Some of our guests feel dizzy in the nanny's room. The air and energy are different up here. During the very first tour I gave, I leaned over to pick up the Brander family picture on the nanny's bed, and I felt like I did a complete somersault! I had to steady myself quickly and pretend nothing had happened in front of my guests. The very first time I was in the house by myself, I went to the nanny's room to get something. Although I had already been back and forth several times across the small room, when I was leaving, it felt like I walked through a spider web. The belief is that when you have this feeling, you've walked through a ghost. So, I quickly gathered what I needed and came back downstairs.

One summer, the air conditioning went out in the upstairs of the house. We were truly "period authentic" during this time, as volunteers and guests alike suffered from the oppressive heat in the upstairs rooms. The thermostat for the upper floors is located at the top of the third-story stairs, right outside the nursery and nanny's room. When I got to the house, I went up to check to make sure the heat wasn't on accidentally. It's dark at the top of those stairs, as the windows are on opposite ends of the third floor. So, I mumbled to myself that I couldn't see anything and pulled out my phone to use the flashlight. I checked the settings, and they were as they should be. When I went downstairs, Gerry asked if I checked another certain setting, which I hadn't, so I came back up. This time, when I reached the top of the stairs, the nursery light was turned on, lighting up the area of the thermostat. That light had not been on when I had just come up a few minutes earlier. I know I didn't turn it on because I had used my flashlight. I stopped, looked around and then thanked the nanny or the child who had turned the light on for me, knowing that I would be coming back up.

My friend Kelly Parker was at the house with me one day, and the security camera in the nursery had fallen, so we went up to fix it. It's precariously mounted to the top of a quilt frame, held on by a ribbon, so it often slips down. We worked on it, cutting a new piece of ribbon, tying it tightly so it would stay. Once we were sure it wasn't going to fall, we turned and walked toward the door. We were only a few feet away when we both heard a loud thud behind us. We looked at each other, knowing the camera had fallen, but when we turned around, it was still securely in place! We never figured out what made the noise.

Corner of the nursery. *Author's collection.*

Ann told me the story of taking a young couple up to the nursery during a tour. When they got up there, the man started gasping for breath. She thought he was having a heart attack. He got as far as the landing and said he couldn't go any farther. Indicating the nanny's room, he said, "There's death in that room. Can you not smell it?" Ann said no but asked what it smelled like. He said ash. She explained to him that there was a fireplace behind the wall and that maybe the dampness was creating the smell. He said no—it was death. He asked her what that room was used for. She told him it was the nanny's room, and several children had died in the house. It was possible they died in that room, especially the younger ones, who would've stayed close to the nanny. He said he couldn't go any farther and went back downstairs. Recently during another tour, a man got very nauseated in the nursery and had to leave the house. Gerry added that she's had several visitors throw up while visiting the third floor.

One of the most perplexing mysteries we've had at the house during my time there involves a piece of clothing. When we give tours, we dress in traditional colonial clothes, so when Cindy started volunteering, she needed an outfit. We were able to find her a chemise and a skirt, but she needed a vest. She and I looked in various closets but couldn't find one. Lastly, we looked in the nursery closet, which has a good number of colonial clothes. I found a vest, but it was small. Cindy made it work, but it was uncomfortable. As she continued to volunteer at the house, other women helped look for a vest, but no one could find one. One day, Cindy came to the house and went up to the nursery to look through the clothes one last time. When she opened the closet door, there was a vest, hanging perpendicular to the other clothes, as if someone had pulled it out and hung it so you could see the entire front. She looked at it. It seemed to be her size, and when she tried it on, it fit perfectly. And it even matched the skirt we had found for her. She asked around to see who had found it, but no one knew anything about it.

The other volunteers had also searched that closet earlier. I even called a former volunteer who worked with our clothes to see if she, by chance, had brought it, but she said no. To this day, we have no idea where the vest came from. Gerry feels it was Belinda. We do feel the house calls to people it wants there, so we just assumed it wanted to make sure Cindy had the clothes she needed. Our answer to this, as well as anything else unexplained, is always, "It's just Ferry!"

A funny incident happened one night when a group of us were at the house waiting for a paranormal team. There was a mix-up on the dates, so the team wasn't coming until the following weekend. Since we were already there, we figured we would do a mini investigation ourselves. It was Cindy, her friend Danielle Mitchell, my friend Kelly and I. We ended up in the nursery. We had an EMF reader with us, which picks up electromagnetic energy. It is believed that if a spirit is near, the electromagnetic levels rise, setting off the device through a series of lights from green to red. Phones will set off this device, so we had it placed away from where we were sitting. We were mostly talking among ourselves, but randomly, the EMF would dance around from green to yellow. We also had an ovilus app on our phones. The ovilus wrote out and spoke words or phrases from the spirits. We weren't necessarily asking questions, but the ovilus was displaying seemingly random words that night. We had been up there for about thirty minutes when suddenly the ovilus displayed "nose ring." We stopped talking and looked at one another. Immediately, Danielle stood up, said, "Nope!" and headed toward the door. Until that moment, the rest of us hadn't even noticed that she had a nose ring, much less said anything about it. Her quick reaction made us laugh, but it couldn't have been a coincidence that the app said this very specific phrase that directly applied to her. We have found that some of our more "traditional" spirits make it known that they don't like tattoos or extra piercings, or perhaps they were fascinated by this jewelry that wasn't common in their time. Either way, this quickly ended our session in the nursery.

The third floor is another area of the house where I ask permission before I come up. Although her duties ended well over a century ago, this is still the nanny's domain, where she had been given the great responsibility of taking care of the children. Knowing that she is protective of these rooms and doesn't like people to be up there, I always ask if I can come up, and then I explain why I need to be there. Although I'm unable to see her, I try not to linger so as to be respectful of her space and not interfere with what she needs to do to properly care for the children.

The spirits from the time of the Civil War seem to be the most active and most prevalent at Ferry Plantation. Perhaps this is due to the stress, anxiety, worry and grief brought on by the war, sickness and devastating loss. That energy seems to remain and presents itself in the spirit form of the people who experienced these strong emotions firsthand. We sometimes sense their grief, physical pain and symptoms of their illnesses. But we also experience laughter, singing and the playful innocence of children. They are a reminder and true representation of the time in which they lived.

OLD DONATION FARM

We're here, you know. All the time. You can talk to us and think about us.
It doesn't have to be sad or scary.
—*Alice Sebold,* The Lovely Bones

CHARLES BARNETT

The narrow spit of land that juts out into the western branch of the Lynnhaven River has been given many names over the years: Ferry Plantation, the Ferry, Ferry Farm, Ferry Landing, Ferry Plantation at the Old Court House, Ferry Plain and Church Quarter. In 1896, when Charles Barnett purchased the property, it was known as Old Donation Farm. The name comes from Old Donation Episcopal Church, which sits less than a mile from the Ferry house. Old Donation was named in recognition of Reverend Robert Dixon, who donated part of his estate in 1733 for the building of the church that was also to be used as a school for orphaned boys. Historic records indicate that Anthony Walke I paid for the construction of the church.

Charles Mitchell Barnett was born in Edinburgh, Scotland, on September 22, 1870. Living in a small apartment, he was educated as a choir boy at Edinburgh Cathedral. In 1887, he immigrated to Canada, where he began his employment with the Grand Trunk Railway. He soon moved to Mexico, where he rose in the ranks of the Mexican Central and Mexican International Railroads. By 1895, Charles had become manager for the Tampico Terminal

Old Donation Episcopal Church. *Author's collection.*

Company, working with the steamers that traveled between England, New York, Baltimore and Mexico. In 1896, he moved to Norfolk, Virginia, as secretary of the South Atlantic Export Company.

Amid his international travels, Charles found himself in rural Spencer County, Indiana, where he met Stella Crowder. Stella was a farmer's daughter, and she married Charles in Dallas, Texas, on March 1, 1894. This may have been where Charles developed his passionate dream of farming and country living. When Charles and Stella moved to Virginia, they bought the 520-plus-acre Old Donation Farm. While also building a home at 521 Fairfax Avenue in the Ghent area of Norfolk, Charles was able to finally fulfill his dream of becoming a farmer. Strawberries, cabbage, wheat and spinach were the major crops grown. Due to his extensive traveling, he maintained the farm with the help of his friend and manager, James Cary (J.C.) Hudgins.

The year following the move to Virginia, Charles became involved with the coal trade, especially in connection with steam shipping. He also quickly integrated into the Norfolk community by joining business and civic societies, as well as becoming the director of the Norfolk Chamber of Commerce. He also became consul for Denmark, Uruguay, Nicaragua, Costa Rica and Paraguay during this time. In 1908, Charles became the president of the Chesapeake and Ohio Coal and Coke Company in

Charles and Stella Barnett's wedding photo in 1894. *Courtesy of the Friends of Ferry Plantation House.*

New York City. His continued success led him to become an authority in the shipping, coal and transportation industry. He was internationally recognized as an expert and was called to testify in more than one thousand cases involving ships and shipping disputes. Some of these cases resulted in awards of millions of dollars.

An article in the December 1903 *American Syren and "Shipping" Illustrated* featured the up-and-coming Charles M. Barnett. After listing his accomplishments to date, the reporter made mention of his character:

> *Personally very modest, Mr. Barnett is appreciated in Norfolk none the less on the account and is as popular in social circles as he is esteemed and respected in the business world. He is, in fact, regarded as the coming man of that section of the South in shipping and coal matters, having attained his eminent position by the energy and hard work that promise him much greater progress.*

The *National Cyclopedia of American Biography* also described Charles Barnett:

> *Despite his affability and personal charm, he was by nature reserved. A scholarly man, his reading covered a wide range of interests. He had an extraordinary memory, in which he stored vast information, and an analytical mind of great power and capacity. He was noted as a mathematician. People came to him for advice and counsel, and he was ever ready to help those faced with perplexing problems, which he simplified by his grasp and insight. He was deeply devoted to his family and his circle of friends. In religion he was an Episcopalian.*

Charles Barnett was instrumental in the reconstruction of Old Donation Episcopal Church, which had burned and fallen into disrepair. In 1915, Charles and Reverend Benjamin Dey White secured a $7,000 bank loan using Charles's business connections in New York. The efforts of Charles, serving as a vestryman, and fellow church members allowed the church to be rebuilt and develop a congregation once again.

Charles Mitchell Barnett. *Courtesy of the Friends of Ferry Plantation House.*

Charles continued to have great success in the shipping industry, right up to his unexpected death on April 26, 1940. He suffered a fatal heart attack at the Waldorf Astoria Hotel in New York City. Ironically, this is where he would frequently dine on the famous Lynnhaven Bay oysters, brought up north from his very own backyard. The oysters were also shipped to the Oyster Bar at Grand Central Station for many years. The Barnetts were known to host and enjoy elaborate oyster roasts on the banks of the Lynnhaven River at their Old Donation Farm.

STELLA CROWDER BARNETT

Stella Crowder was born on September 6, 1862, in Spencer County, Indiana. Charles Barnett was visiting Indiana when he met the Crowder family, fell in love and married Stella in 1894. Charles and Stella were living in Mexico City when their first child, Jean (Jeannie), was born in 1895. The young family came back to the United States in 1896, settling in Virginia, where Charles established his residence and business relations in Norfolk. As mentioned earlier, the Barnetts maintained a house in the Ghent section of Norfolk, but they also purchased Old Donation Farm to fulfill Charles's dream of becoming a farmer. Once in Virginia, Charles and Stella grew their family with the birth of Charles Jr. (called Carlos) in 1900 and Joseph in 1901.

Tragedy struck the Barnett household at Old Donation Farm in October 1912. At the time, Charles was away on a business trip. The story is told that Stella was returning from a trip to Europe and requested her favorite mushroom soup. Mushrooms were gathered from the farm, as was customary, and the meal was prepared and served. The family tasted the soup and then pushed it away, saying it didn't taste right. Stella claimed it was fine and ate all of hers. Stella soon fell ill. To the family's horror, they realized that a poisonous toadstool had made its way into the soup. They carried Stella upstairs to her room (the Green Room), where she lay dying. It is said that twelve-year-old Carlos jumped on his horse and rode to get the doctor. Stella was treated but suffered for three days in her Old Donation home before

Old Donation Farm, 1898. *Courtesy of the Friends of Ferry Plantation House.*

the decision was made to take her to Protestant Hospital in Norfolk. The October 12, 1912 *Virginian Pilot and Norfolk Landmark* noted:

> *When brought to the hospital she was suffering from violent congestion and the physician held out very little hope at the time, as the case had advanced too far before she was brought to the hospital, and her death followed at 6 o'clock yesterday afternoon.*

Stella Barnett's funeral was held at Old Donation Farm (Ferry Plantation) the following Monday, October 14. She would later be buried at her family's cemetery plot in Indiana. It is interesting and a bit concerning to note that wild mushrooms still grow on the property of Ferry Plantation. We even have the Barnett family recipe for Stella's mushroom soup.

CORA CROWDER BARNETT

Charles was at a loss with Stella's passing, especially with three young children to raise. His work frequently took him away from home, so he wrote to Stella's sister, Cora, who was currently serving as a nurse and stenographer in India, to see if she would come help him take care of the children. The Barnett family have shared the letters that were written between Charles and Cora during this time. On October 13, 1912, not yet knowing the cause of Stella's death, Cora wrote:

> *Dear dear Charlie,*
>
> *O dear, O dear. What can I say? I feel broken hearted and empty—what must you feel and the children and mother. Dear people. Stella not there. My, my. Life isn't worth living. I wish I had gone home sooner. I wish I had. I didn't realize how much I could miss her.…She has always been so healthy. I was prepared for anything but losing her. I thought and hoped I would not be the one left. Poor you and poor children. Poor indeed! You will all be nearer and dearer to us than ever, though we can't fill the gap. I know how much she was to you.…I wonder what could have happened. Surely no heart trouble—and I wonder if that horse ran away with her again, or some other accident. Dear, dear. What could it have been and why couldn't it have been someone less needed.…I feel so sorry for my selfish self that I haven't any sister and most of all, no Stella!*

Cora and Stella Crowder Barnett. *Courtesy of the Friends of Ferry Plantation House.*

Charles and Cora seemed to have had a friendly relationship, despite the twelve-year age difference between her and Stella. On April 26, 1894, two months after marrying Stella, Charles wrote a letter to his new sister-in-law:

> *My Dear Cora:*
>
> *It seems funny, and almost like taking liberties, to say my dear to someone (you feel and know is dear to you) whom you have never met. But I should think it will be all right in this instance, and I hope you will read these few lines with as much pleasure as I'm anticipating in the receipt of a letter from my new, and dear, sister.... Were you surprised and disappointed when you learned that Stella had taken such a serious step as marry an old man you didn't know, or were you glad and may I expect to see you over here this summer?...I had hoped to have come over for Stella and make friends with you all but the inexorable railroads...it's hard to be your own boss when subject to the whims of these railroad people.*

Agreeing to Charles's request, Cora left her duties in India and, after several months of travel, joined her sister's widower and children at Old Donation Farm. She stayed with the family and helped raise the three children. On March 1, 1914, she and Charles married, twenty years to the day that he married Stella. I always say on my tours that Charles wanted to remember only one anniversary date.

In October 1914, Lewis Walke made a trip to Princess Anne County to visit his ancestral home. On October 20, 1914, he wrote:

> *Upon arriving to Shelton Station we found that the name "The Ferry" was not known by those of whom we asked directions. However, Mr. Hoggard* [real estate agent] *had told us that the place is now owned by Mr. C.M. Barnett....When we reached Old Donation Church...he told us that the road to the right of the church led to Mr. Barnett's place.*

He continued on October 21, 1914:

> *We went first to "Springfield" and then on to the "Ferry." Mr. Barnett was not at home, but Mrs. Barnett* [Cora] *was most kind in showing us everything which we wanted to see and afterwards in serving tea for us. She is enthusiastic about the old place and was much interested in learning that it had been called "The Ferry" and in other things which I could tell her about it. She told us that the neighborhood tradition says that the house was formerly the jail and Third Courthouse of Princess Anne County....We were shown the iron bars to the window of this room.*

In addition to embracing the historical value of the home, Cora continued the family tradition of entertaining from the 1920s to the 1940s. The *Norfolk Sun* published the article "Colonial Days Again in Princess Anne" on May 17, 1931. The article described how more than one thousand people attended the play *Two Mile Tree*, which was performed on the landside porch of "the old Barnette Place, now Old Donation Farm." Mary Sinton Leitch wrote this play based on the American Revolution for the sixth annual Woman's Club's May Festival.

Eventually, Charles's work took him and Cora to New York City, but the couple frequently returned to visit Virginia. Friend and joint owner James (J.C.) Hudgins ran the farm in their absence. After Charles's death in 1940, his son Charles Jr. (Carlos) inherited and ran the farm for many years with Hudgins. A descendant of the Hudgins family, Carl Hellstrom Jr., told the volunteers at Ferry Plantation that Cora would still come down to visit the farm for about a month each summer after they permanently moved to New York. He said she would get up early in the morning and hike all around Old Donation Farm, sometimes not returning back to the house until late afternoon. He described how one time Cora invited them to come visit her in New York:

The following summer we took her up on it. We stayed with her a week, maybe 10 days. She took us all over New York. She took us to West Point, The Bronx Zoo, Grand Central Station, the Statue of Liberty, The Empire State Building, all of the things. She liked to walk us to death! We couldn't hardly keep up with her. We were like 16–17 years old....She told us about traveling to Mongolia on camelback, back around the turn of the century. She was a nurse. She had a real nice apartment with stuff she'd collected all around the world. This was about 1952, I guess, was the last time I saw her. She was in her late 70s then, about 76–77 years old. She was one wiry woman....And she was always talking, telling you stories about something...Cora, she was such a nice lady, just as nice as could be.

Cora Crowder Barnett passed away in 1971. Ferry Plantation has had many Barnett visitors to the house who fondly remember "Auntie Co." In May 2002, there was a Barnett Family Reunion at Ferry Plantation, including an oyster roast down by the river. Several family members recalled visiting

Barnett gravestone in Richardson Cemetery, Rockport, Indiana. *Courtesy of the Friends of Ferry Plantation House.*

their grandfather Charles and Aunt Cora at Old Donation Farm before the couple moved to New York.

Charles Barnett was devoted to both of his wives and is buried in between the two sisters at the Richardson Family Cemetery in Rockport, Indiana.

SPIRITS OF THE BARNETTS

As I write this section, I'm sitting in the Green Room at Ferry Plantation House. This is the room where the family brought Stella Barnett after she was poisoned by the toadstool in her mushroom soup. She lay dying here for three days before she was taken to the hospital in Norfolk. She died on October 11, 1912, and her funeral was held here at Ferry. A basket of mushrooms sits on the hearth in this room. A picture of Stella and Cora is displayed on the mantel.

In her book *Ghosts, Witches, and Weird Tales of Virginia Beach*, Belinda reported guests' sightings of a woman who looks like Stella. She appears in the Green Room, going about her business. When these occurrences were first reported, the volunteers at Ferry did not yet know Stella's history, nor had they seen a picture of her. Others have heard sounds of choking or moaning coming from this same room.

Cody told the story about a volunteer who was sitting in the library and suddenly said, "The sister on the right's corset is too tight." He looked at her strangely and wasn't sure he heard her correctly. He asked her to repeat what she had just said. She repeated the same sentence, while looking up at the picture of Stella and Cora on the mantel. Then it made sense. Cora was on the left; Stella was on the right. If you suffer from mushroom poisoning, you have heavy congestion and difficulty breathing. Was Stella telling this volunteer that she needed to loosen her corset to be able to breathe?

As Stella was known for her love of entertaining, socializing and traveling, it is no surprise that she is one of our more outgoing spirits. We have been told that she is still forever the good hostess and continues to make sure the house is taken care of. One of our volunteers, Ruthe, has had guests tell her that Stella follows her around the house. Ruthe was instrumental in the Barnett family research, so it would make sense that Stella feels a connection with her.

When Ambrosia Matthews came to the house for a tour with her children, we were walking into the parlor, and she put her arms around her youngest child and reminded him not to touch anything. I told her that we are a hands-on museum and that most things were okay to touch. She then explained that she had already been told three times by the spirit of a matronly woman in a white blouse that she needed to take her children upstairs to the nursery, that they were not supposed to be in the formal downstairs rooms of the house. She was also very emphatic that Ambrosia made sure that her children did not touch her fan. The white blouse makes me think this could have been Stella. As we continued the tour and came into the Green Room, I remembered that we have a feathered fan hanging up in her open closet. Is this what Stella was insistent that the children not touch?

On Ambrosia's visit in 2022, when we were in the Green Room, I explained that this was where Stella lay dying. She said she felt like someone wasn't there when this happened. She was correct because Charles was away on business, and Cora was in India. When Port City Paranormal was here doing a paranormal investigation, they caught a woman singing while "baking a pumpkin pie." Another paranormal group captured a voice saying, "Our sister is in the house." Do these voices belong to Stella as she was going about everyday life and referring to her sister, Cora?

Cody told the story of one night after a particularly late paranormal investigation. He was finally able to go to sleep and was lying on his air mattress in front of the fireplace in the library. He said that he was just about asleep when he felt his body rise up and back down on the mattress. Then there was a laugh. Once more, his body rose up and down. Another volunteer in the next room yelled over to him that they didn't know what was going on, but someone found it hilarious. Cody was convinced it was the spirit of Stella, stepping on the end of his air mattress making him rise up and down and then laughing.

A medium visiting the house claimed that Stella's son is still in the Green Room. We have had several paranormal groups receive the name Joseph in the house. Joseph was Charles's and Stella's youngest child. *The Oddity Files* filmed its investigation at Ferry in 2013 and caught the name Joseph on a spirit box in the Green Room. (A spirit box is a device through which the spirits can speak with their own voice.) They claimed to hear a boy screaming while an orb danced around them. While in that room, they also asked Stella if she was happy when her husband married her sister. They heard a woman replying, "I wasn't."

One evening, while I was waiting for a paranormal team, I went outside to take some pictures of the house. Later that night, I was looking through the photos and noticed something inside the courthouse. When I zoomed

Shore of Old Donation Farm, 1909. *Courtesy of Wink Simpson.*

in on the window, I could clearly see a woman walking from the courthouse into the dining room. She was wearing a white blouse with a large collar and a dark skirt, and her brown hair was pulled up into a bun on the top of her head. She looked exactly like the women in the oyster roast pictures we have from 1909. Due to the dress and hairstyle, I believe this was the spirit of Stella, although I was a bit unnerved because I had just walked out of that room minutes earlier.

The spirit of Charles Barnett is known to still be in his beloved home at Old Donation Farm as well, although he tends to be more reserved than his outgoing first wife. Sometimes when young female guests come into the house wearing a crop top, they will feel a poke on their stomach. This has been attributed to Charles, letting the young lady know that he doesn't feel her attire is appropriate to wear in his house. Ambrosia once had the feeling that a spirit was trying to rub off her tattoos. She felt like they were viewed as inappropriate. Could this also have been Charles Barnett, continuing to remind the women who enter his house what is acceptable and proper?

While there aren't many interactions with the spirit of Cora, there is a strong sense that she also remains in the house. Cody explained that Cora was more quiet in life, so it makes sense that we have more interactions with Stella since she was, and continues to be, the more outgoing sister.

THE HUDGINS/HOWREN FAMILY

When Charles and Cora moved to New York City, they left Old Donation Farm in the care of James Cary (J.C.) Hudgins, who owned 50 percent of the farm. When Charles passed away in 1940, he left his portion of the farm to his son Charles (Carlos) Jr. Sadly, Carlos died soon after in 1947. J.C. Hudgins then purchased the 425-acre farm in 1948. J.C.'s daughter, Ethel Howren, would be the last resident of Ferry Plantation House, passing away in 1983.

In 2013, Hudgins family members Carl Hellstrom Jr. and Joey Day met with Belinda Nash and other volunteers to share their family history and memories of growing up on the Ferry farm. They were half brothers, and both were grandsons of J.C. Hudgins. They first explained how J.C. Hudgins was also known by the name of Bill Jones. They described the house as not having the front and back porches at that time and fondly remembered playing croquet out on the lawn. They explained that the driveway came to the landside part of the house and made a teardrop shape in front. They

Ferry Plantation House, 1955. *Courtesy of the Friends of Ferry Plantation House.*

Bill Jones (James Carey Hudgins) in *Farm Magazine. Courtesy of the Friends of Ferry Plantation House.*

remembered that the old windmill's grinding stone was on the property for many years. It was removed for a time but then donated back to the Friends of Ferry Plantation House by the Hudgins family. They shared that the Barnetts had left some furniture in the house, including a sideboard and a large captain's desk.

The half brothers described their grandfather's farm as producing mostly kale, collards, spinach and feed corn. But they also grew turnips, potatoes, snap beans, cantaloupe, alfalfa, soybeans, cucumbers and strawberries. They explained how J.C. would send the produce to Baltimore, Philadelphia and New York. They showed the picture of J.C. holding up corn for a picture that appeared in *Farm Magazine*.

Carl and Joel explained how there was a small store on the property for the African Americans. They described it as little more than a toolshed, but they remembered the Dr Pepper and Pepsi men coming around to stock it. The men also described an area they called the Indian Pit. They found arrowheads there and described it as being about thirty feet long and ten feet deep. They claim that one of their family members found an old Native American stone axe in the same area. They also found Native American pottery near the dam at the back of the property.

They spoke of the graveyard that was located in an area that extended out into the Lynnhaven River. They said there was a spot of land that their father would never let them plow over, claiming that an unmarked grave lay below. Their mother had always said that Stella Barnett was buried there, but when Charles permanently moved to New York, he had her reburied in her family plot in Indiana. They remember Jean Barnett coming to visit Charles and Cora when they were little. Carl was the one who went to New York City to visit Cora when he was a teenager.

J.C.'s daughter, Ethel Hudgins Howren, was the last person to live in the Ferry Plantation House. She was very active in Old Donation Episcopal Church and became the first woman elected to the vestry. She donated land to the church with an agreement that a labyrinth would be built, which was accomplished through an Eagle Scout project. Jo Howren, Ethel's daughter-in-law, became one of the first voices to speak out to save Ferry Plantation House after Ethel passed away in 1983. The adjoining neighborhood to Ferry is aptly named J.C. Hudgins Shores.

SPIRIT EXPERIENCES WITH THE HUDGINS/HOWRENS

In their talk with Belinda, Joel and Carl each shared a paranormal experience that they had at the house. Joel explained how when he and his wife were dating back in the late 1950s, they were having a picnic near the house with some friends. Afterward, he, his wife and one of their friends decided to walk down to Ferry. They knew that Ethel was away on a trip, so no one would be home. As they walked closer to the house, they saw someone inside, moving from window to window on the first floor. He explained that even back then, the ghost stories about the house were popular. He said that his wife turned around and ran so fast that he couldn't catch her.

Carl told the story about how one time when he was standing outside the house, he saw a light up on the third story. He said it looked like a candle and moved back and forth between the two windows, like someone was pacing. The third floor is the nursery, so could it have been the nanny walking back and forth by candlelight with a sick child?

Belinda once spoke with other family members who used to come and visit back in the 1970s. The cousins used to sleep in the room that is now our gift shop. Each night, they would see two women working and walking in front of the fireplace. The room seemed very familiar to them. This was an unsettling experience for the girls, as all three had seen the apparitions multiple times. Could this have been the McIntosh sisters who shared this room during the Civil War?

In 1996, Belinda spoke with a woman who knew about some unusual experiences that happened near the house. During 1980–81, Ethel Howren was no longer able to stay at the Old Donation House and moved into a condominium. The family didn't rent out the house but had caregivers stay

Ferry Plantation House in 1954. *Courtesy of the Friends of Ferry Plantation House.*

while Ethel was away. Many unexplained things happened at the house during this time. They had heard the stories of Grace Sherwood and thought that maybe it was she who walked around the house after dark. They were reportedly spooked by this lady in white. They also claimed to have visits from the "old black servant" who we now know to be Henry. He was seen at the same time night after night doing some sort of chores before passing through the pantry door. They also claimed that two children were always in the house. Perhaps these were Bessie and Eric?

The woman also told the story about a time when the same caregivers were leaving the property. Brick pillars originally stood at the entrance of the road leading to Ferry. As they were driving out, their car inexplicably stalled right at the pillars. Another time, a white wispy form was in front of the car as it stalled again. On the third occasion, a black cat came out of nowhere near the brick pillars and was spooked. As soon as the cat ran off, the car stalled once again. Each time, they were able to easily start the car again, and each occurrence took place on a Saturday. It was almost as if the spirits at the house did not want them to leave, knowing that the time was soon coming when the house would stand vacant and vulnerable to vandals for the next thirteen years.

RESTORATION

This is a happenin' place.
—Belinda Nash

THE FIGHT TO SAVE HISTORY

The oldest part of the iconic Ferry Plantation House has stood proudly for nearly 250 years. It survived a revolution, civil war, multiple generations of families, death, celebrations and modernization. Sadly, it was this last stage that almost caused its demise. When Ethel Howren passed away in 1983, the house stood vacant, exposed to vandals, thrill-seekers and bored teenagers who dared one another to go inside the "haunted house." The years-long battle over what to do with the old home nearly brought about its destruction through neglect, ruin and decay.

Ferry Plantation House remained in the Howren family until it was sold in 1986 to developers Reid & Womack, which formed Old Donation Farm Associates. In April 1987, Old Donation Farm was created. In July 1987, the 3.9-acre site was rezoned as a Historical and Cultural Overlay District. During this time, archaeologists from the Colonial Williamsburg Foundation conducted an excavation on Ferry Plantation land, focusing on the remains of a structure near the current house. In the *Virginian-Pilot* article "18th Century Artifacts Found at Ferry Farm," Marc Davis wrote that the archaeologists believed their brick foundation site to be that of the early eighteenth-century tavern that stood next to the courthouse. They uncovered more than fifty-three thousand artifacts, the largest collection of eighteenth-century artifacts found to date, since that area of land had been relatively untouched for two hundred years. They knew that growth was coming, as the developers planned to build thirty-nine houses on this peninsula. Colonial Williamsburg was given permission to conduct the dig before the site was destroyed by the upcoming construction. Some of the artifacts they found include spoons, broken wine bottles, a punch bowl and other ceramics, copper shoe buckles and even Spanish coins.

"A Study of the Ferry Plantation House," written by Fairlamb Sadler & Whitehead Architects and Burkhart/Thomas Architecture, explained how this excavation's "evidence of fine quality porcelain, bone handled utensils and a number of handsome brass buckles would indicate the owner's wealth and prestige." Robert Hunter, in charge of the dig, wrote to owner Donald Reid on September 15, 1987:

> *The archaeological materials recovered represent one of the best preserved assemblages of 18th century artifacts yet excavated in the tidewater area of the Middle Atlantic region.... Our historical research has indicated that Anthony Walke was the largest landowner and wealthiest man in Princess Anne County.*

In Brenda Harris's 1995 article "At Home: Old Donation Farm, Virginia Beach Where Past and Present Nicely Blend," she described that in 1987, the residents of the nearby Pembroke Meadows neighborhood circulated petitions trying to block any development near the historic "Ferry Farm Manor House." They were unsuccessful. In 1989, the Virginia Beach Arts Center held the title to the house. However, when it realized it would cost close to $3 million to restore the home, the title was transferred back to the Old Donation Farm Associates. Harris went on to explain how there was confusion over the current ownership since the title was "clouded." A private citizen planned to buy the house, but residents protested, citing the subdivision covenants that said the "manor house" would never be used as a personal residence. They did, however, support the house becoming a museum. Harris described how the delays concerning the use of the house caused more deterioration with weeds invading the home, vandalism and extensive disrepair.

In 1994, the Virginia Beach City Council agreed to uphold the 1987 conditions that Ferry Plantation House would not become a private dwelling.

Ferry Plantation House at the beginning of restoration in the late 1990s. *Courtesy of the Friends of Ferry Plantation House.*

In January 1995, Friends of Ferry Plantation House Inc. (FOFPH) was formed. Jo Howren, daughter-in-law to Ethel Howren, Ferry's last resident, became president and was instrumental in the fight to preserve the house. In the article "Championing Historic Home, Woman Invokes Author Cather," author Greg Goldfard quoted Jo Howren as saying, "We can't get another Ferry Plantation House. We've got to save this one." The article described how the Friends wanted to restore the deteriorating home, open it as a museum and offer tours to the public.

In the July 1996 article "An Historic Revival After Years of Neglect, the Ferry Plantation House Will Be Renovated, Preserving 300 Years of Local History," Mary Reid Barrow wrote about the struggle over the fate of this historic home. She explained how recent actions have revived hope that this site will be preserved as a symbol of three centuries of local Virginia Beach history. She quoted then City Councilwoman Barbara M. Henley, who had written a paper as a graduate student at Old Dominion University about the importance of saving this home: "To me this is the most significant historical site in Virginia Beach. There's been something happening here the whole time!" The current investors, Hickory Properties, agreed to deed Ferry Plantation House to the city. It also purchased two lots from the city for $68,550 that would ultimately become the seed money for restoring the house. The article also explained how the home was historically known as "Ferry Farm," but the Friends chose to change the name to "Ferry Plantation" to distinguish it from George Washington's birthplace.

In this same article, Jo Howren explained how the first part of the plan called for the hiring of a historical architect using a $1,000 grant that the Friends received. Henley added that the next step would be to restore the outside "so that it would be aesthetically pleasing to the neighbors." She continued, "The house is certainly old and historic, but the site is where the real historic significance is and it should be available to the public."

In October 1996, the Virginia Beach City Council unanimously approved the plans for the Friends to restore and maintain Ferry Plantation House, with the City of Virginia Beach being the owner. Surrounded by the thirty-nine new upscale homes on this thirty-three-acre peninsula, Brenda Harris concluded her article this way: "Old Donation Farm is a secluded waterfront neighborhood where the past meets the present in a very visible way. The manor house gives a clue to what life was like in Princess Anne County in the past, and the luxurious modern homes tell us about life in Virginia Beach in the 1990s."

RESTORATION

Now the real work began. The Friends were able to start the restoration with the seed money given by the city. They also had grant money to hire a historic architect. In 1998, Mary Reid Barrow wrote another article titled "Architects Examine Ferry Plantation for Restoration." She wrote that ten architects from the Historic Committee of the Virginia Society of American Institute of Architects made a point of meeting once a year at a historic site in need of work. That particular year, they were working at Ferry Plantation. Upon their inspection, they found that part of the house was held together by wooden pegs, not nails. The architects explained how the house was both old and new, its development taking place over the past 175 years. They advised the Friends to take the renovation slowly, thoroughly researching how the house developed over the years. They suggested finding out as much as they could about the property and families who lived there, as well as garnering community support in its restoration. A local community college interior design class would assist with suggestions for the interior, based on their research of period design. Jo Howren described the preservation process: "It's a little bit like a tsunami. And we're going to ride it to the point where the house is stabilized and open again."

The November 1999 article by Barrow, "Architects Build Success into Ferry Plantation Renovation Effort," announced that the second floor of the Ferry Plantation House had been fully renovated and leased to the nonprofit group American Institute of Architects (AIA), Hampton Roads Chapter. This fulfilled one of the Friends' goals to rent the second floor to a nonprofit group while restoring the first floor as a local history center. Having the AIA group housed on site, they were able to protect the house by reporting any maintenance issues immediately and reducing the risk of vandalism. The rent would also go toward the restoration of the remaining rooms.

Frequent newspaper articles were published with updates on the renovation of this historic home. Belinda Nash explained how they were able to date the house from paint samples. The middle section of the house was dated to 1830 and the newer west wing addition to 1850. It seemed that throughout the generations, the families of Ferry didn't scrape off previous layers of paint and wallpaper before adding new ones, giving us a historical timeline that has proved invaluable to reconstructing the house's development. In another article, Belinda, then treasure of FOFPH, requested that Ferry receive a preservation grant due to the ferry system that dated the land back to 1642. With that grant money, the Friends hoped to replace the oyster shell stucco that previously covered soft exterior bricks on the house.

Along with articles regarding the house's restoration progress, there were those that featured the historical education the volunteers at Ferry offered to the community. An article in August 2003 featured Belinda giving a talk and demonstration to thirty children who learned about Grace Sherwood, colonial gardens and herbs, how to churn butter and what chores children were responsible for, including gathering eggs and chopping wood. A later article described the Historic Ferry Plantation House's May Day event, which included dancing, English food and gifts. This fundraiser included a visit from Manteo's Elizabethan Gardens' queen, her court, dancers and a procession of bagpipers. The article ended by announcing an upcoming Queen's Tea, hosted by Belinda and the Friends volunteers. Ferry Plantation tea parties were a profitable source of fundraising for the home. Each event had a different theme, and while the ladies enjoyed their afternoon tea sitting at nice table settings in fancy clothes, paper and paint were peeling off the walls behind them. However, everyone pretended not to notice. The proceeds from each event went directly back into the restoration of the house.

Top: Magical Tea, March 2005—one of the many fundraising events for Ferry Plantation. *Courtesy of the Friends of Ferry Plantation House.*

Bottom: View of Ferry Plantation's Celtic garden from the third floor. *Author's collection.*

In the April 15, 2005 article "Ferry Plantation Researchers Plan 1830s Garden," Patricia Neleski reported on the colonial herb and kitchen garden that was designed and created for the landside of the house. Belinda, now museum director, described the four beds surrounded by a central brick walk: "Each bed contains different plants: kitchen herbs, medicinal herbs, flavoring herbs and the 'cash crops' of tobacco and cotton for the museum's educational class." Ferry's history always seems to surface, even when focusing on the gardens. Belinda said, "No matter where we dig here, we find artifacts." She leaned down to a freshly dug bed and pulled out a pottery shard. "I have a dish full of these from the project."

The front of Ferry Plantation House exhibits a beautiful Celtic garden. Belinda had this garden designed and created in the late 1990s. Ann Henley has faithfully maintained our gardens since the early 2000s. She described the Celtic garden as having germander on the outside with gardenias in the center. The smaller four gardens use monkey grass as the border with dianthus in the center. Each spring, she and her husband, Al, clean out the gardens, replace plants as needed and keep the beds weeded throughout the summer. We also have an abundance of rosemary growing in the garden next to the side door, in honor and recognition of Grace Sherwood, the legendary Witch of Pungo. We are proud that these gardens are what guests first notice when approaching the house, as they provide a visual insight into colonial life.

Through the Friends' dedication and countless hours of hard work, Ferry Plantation House became designated as part of the following historic registries:

- Historical Register of the City of Virginia Beach, 2003
- State of Virginia Historic Landmarks, 2004
- National Register of Historic Places, 2005

ROSE HALL

While there were lengthy property battles, disputes over the use of the house and the close reality of losing the home in favor of a recreation center, Ferry Plantation was one of the lucky ones to have survived the onslaught of development in Virginia Beach. Not all historic homes fared so well. Historic Rose Hall is an example of one that fell victim to the rapid growth that overtook the city.

In 1712, William Ellegood received a land grant for 615 acres in what is now known as the Great Neck area of Virginia Beach. Stands of pine and oak trees lined the Rose Hall Plantation's shoreline along the Lynnhaven River. The original house burned down in 1820 but was replaced soon after by a Federal-style home on the same foundation. By 2002, only three acres remained of the original property. The rest had been subdivided into housing and businesses according to the article "Historic Virginia Beach Home Up for Sale, Prompting Worry." Matthew Jones described Rose Hall as one of Virginia Beach's oldest homesteads from the eighteenth century, citing that it was built before Thomas Jefferson went to Williamsburg. Ironically, in his 1753 will, Jacob Ellegood left Rose Hall to Colonel Anthony Walke and John Saunders of Pembroke Hall. However, Anthony Walke refused it due to owning Fairfield Plantation at the time. The house was eventually sold to Ellegood's younger son, William.

In his article, Jones wrote that in 2002, the elderly owner of Rose Hall knew she could no longer take care of the house, but she and the neighbors were concerned over losing the home and its heritage. Mary Alexander, a neighbor, said, "There's a whole patch of history missing in Virginia Beach…homes like Rose Hall. They keep tearing them all down." The neighbors wanted to see Rose Hall designated as a historic site. The 2003 article "Fight Continues to Save Beach Home" discussed the extremely high costs of trying to move the home and then renovate it. The total price would be close to $1 million. One of the main concerns was the house's extensive termite damage. They felt it was too far gone to be salvaged.

Rose Hall, 2004. Bricks and pine boards were saved from Rose Hall before its demolition and used in the restoration of Ferry Plantation House. *Courtesy of the Friends of Ferry Plantation House.*

Since Rose Hall couldn't be saved, they did the next best thing. They called Belinda and told her that she had three days to grab as many materials as she could from the old house to use in the renovation at Ferry. Gerry Richter recalled the frantic call from Belinda, saying that they needed to find a truck and head to Rose Hall immediately. They gathered as many people as they could and went to work for three days hauling bricks and salvageable boards. In the end, they transported more than 3,000 bricks and removed 150 heart pine floorboards from Rose Hall's bedrooms. The bricks were stored at Ferry Plantation. Gerry tells how everyone involved had the floorboards stored in attics, garages, sheds and anywhere else they could find space until it was time to use them. In the end, most of the bricks were used as the soldier (outer) bricks that now line Ferry's sidewalk going up to the house from the parking lot. In 2004, the walk was completed and dedicated to Rose Hall by Mayor Meyera Oberndorf.

The pine boards were used to restore the interior of the old courthouse. The floor, stairs, closet and trunk were all renovated using Rose Hall's floorboards. Gerry explained how not many could be saved because most of the house was eaten up by termites. The article "Restoring Fireplace Found at Ferry Plantation House" described how some of the Rose Hall bricks were used to rebuild the fireplace in the old courthouse. Due to modern upgrades through the years, the courthouse had been serving as a 1980s kitchen when the renovations began. The original fireplace was hidden under a staircase and behind modern appliances. When the stairs were moved back to their original location, it was time to rebuild the outer portion of the fireplace and hearth. The interior is original. Since the courthouse dates to the 1700s, Belinda wanted the fireplace restored with old bricks. They decided to use bricks that had been excavated during archaeological digs during the Ferry summer camps, along with bricks from Rose Hall. Belinda is quoted as saying, "Rose Hall's heart will live on here."

The fate of Rose Hall reminded Virginia Beach residents of the loss of another historic home several decades earlier. The last remaining building of the Walke family's "baronial" Fairfield estate was lost to developers in 1972. In her article "Old Fairfield House to Be Demolished," Helen Crist wrote that this small, one-and-a-half-story structure was the last remaining building from the Fairfield era. It was likely an office, lodge or coachman's house that stood alongside the original Fairfield mansion. Despite the developer W.W. Reasor's fight to save the home, the necessary funds were not available. Crist wrote, "And maybe the generations of Walkes,

Opposite: The soldier bricks lining the outer edges of Ferry Plantation's sidewalk were salvaged from Rose Hall. *Author's collection*.

Above: Fairfield Plantation Dependency, circa 1924. This last standing building of the Walke's Fairfield Plantation was torn down in 1972. *Courtesy of Sargeant Memorial Collection, Norfolk Public Library.*

reportedly buried on a little ridge not too far from the house, will stir a little and they'll know when the house goes down." She concluded her article by saying, "And when the little Fairfield house comes crashing down, there will be some who will watch misty-eyed and wonder…'how in the world did this happen?' But others, seeing it go, will say, 'Good riddance. It's no loss—it was old anyway.'"

Many of the historic homes and plantations in Virginia Beach are now just a distant memory as neighborhoods, shopping centers and busy roads stand in their place. While we can understand the financial challenges of trying to save these old houses, it's sad to see their history lost. That's why when I walk up to the front of the Ferry Plantation House, I smile as I walk over the granite stone commemorating Rose Hall. Like Belinda, I'm glad to know that part of Rose Hall will always live on at Ferry.

DISCOVERING SPIRITS THROUGH RESTORATION

Even though Ferry Plantation House sits on an acre and a half of open space in the middle of the Old Donation Farm neighborhood, only fifteen feet out from the house is considered Ferry Plantation property. The rest belongs to the Old Donation Farm Homeowners Association as common ground. The Walke family once owned more than seven thousand acres, and this portion of their estate is now reduced to just fifteen feet. But the house remains! And as we've already seen in previous chapters, the spirits have chosen to stay as well. During the time that the house sat vacant, neighbors and thrill-seekers alike claimed that balls of light danced around the Ferry Plantation roof, even at a time when there was no electricity turned on in the house.

Soon after Belinda Nash and other volunteers started renovating the house, they realized that the house was not truly empty after all. Belinda wrote, "You enter any room and get the feeling that you are not alone. Shortness of breath, heaviness on your chest, signs that someone from the past is trying to contact you. I call those visitors 'soul prints of the past.' They just want their story told." She went on to describe the following experience:

> *I am now all alone in the house and from under the floorboards, faint cries could be heard, as if someone or something were being hurt. Could this be an animal trapped below? The sounds became clearer. I went outside to see if anyone was calling, or if maybe a rusted hinge had made the noise. No one could be found and the hinges got some attention with oil. The sounds came again more muffled but this time it was a man's voice that could be heard. Could it be voices bouncing off the surrounding houses? The chills cause the hair on the back of your neck and arms to raise. Is it my imagination playing tricks on me? Maybe just the wind catching the tree branches just right made the sounds. At this point I felt I should leave but debated putting off my work at the house. At different times as the neighborhood was being built up, strange sounds were reported from under the old house left boarded up and abandoned for twelve years. The sound of chains dragging and heavy doors banging were heard along with cries from the sycamore tree. The iron bars remain on the windows with the shackles and keys, reminders of the old courthouse….The souls of the past have a story to tell and only time can reveal their message.*

The volunteers began embracing the "Hauntingly Historic Ferry Plantation House." Each October, they would host Spirit Tours, which led guests from room to room, hearing stories of true sightings at the house. Guests could then stay until midnight to investigate on their own with the help of a paranormal team. Visitors could also attend the Ferryman's Wake, an interactive comedy about the customs and superstitions surrounding death and marriage since the 1800s. On Halloween, costumed docents told tales of hauntings at the house during the Stroll of the Lost Souls. A mock séance was held, along with psychic readings, and if they dared, guests could choose to stay overnight. Nearly every event involved telling the story of Grace Sherwood, the Witch of Pungo. The flyers for these events at Ferry included the following disclaimer:

> *The spirits in this house are real, and there are no "attractions" added for your entertainment. If you see a shadow, feel a chill, hear a baby cry, or* [feel] *the cat rub up against you, be assured that you have had a real paranormal encounter.*

Later, Spirited Events at the Ferry Plantation House expanded to include paranormal education classes as well as group investigations. Among the myriad articles written about the home's restoration, stories about its hauntings started to make their appearance. In 2005, the *Daily Break* published the article "Things Go Bump in the Night at Eerie House." When arriving at the house for his interview, reporter Roy Bahls and two friends were met at the front door by Belinda in her seven-layer antebellum dress with a hoop skirt and lace cap. She told them, "There are 11 spirits that call this house their home....That's what I've been able to gather from over 70 descriptions of sightings." Belinda described the little girl who is often seen. "She doesn't seem to be sinister but she scares the wits out of people when she shows up, then disappears." Belinda told them how she recently saw a tall shadow going up the first-floor stairway. "It took my breath for a moment. We had the house blessed a few years ago, so we have only good spirits here." During their overnight stay, Bahls wrote about hearing heavy footsteps while in the nursery and then the "scampering of little feet upstairs" in the gift shop.

In 2011, Bob Ruegsegger's article "Ferry Plantation House Shows Its Holiday Spirit" featured the Stroll of the Lost Souls event that the house hosted each October. Belinda explained, "We're a house in mourning through the whole month of October, so we dress in black." Referring to the name of the event, Belinda said, "We know the histories of the families that lived here....In the records, we have the names of lost souls. It's very fitting." Ruegsegger described the sightings of the little girl, Henry and Stella Barnett.

Belinda stated, "It's comforting to know that they're here, that the house is attended and that someone is watching." This annual event brought in money used for the home's restoration and maintenance. Belinda's daughter, Danielle Sheets, concluded with, "We don't jump out and scare people like in a standard spooky haunted house....We just tell them of actual events, and the house just creeps them out."

In the YouTube video "Ferry Plantation, Haunted or Not? You Decide," Danielle told about an experience during the Stroll of the Lost Souls. During their first Halloween event, they shared the history of the Fox sisters and their creation of the séance in 1830, the same year Ferry was built. As part of their presentation, they held a mock séance. A group was seated around a wooden table in the middle of the parlor. During their performance, Danielle said that the table did a quarter turn completely on its own. She said they were around a heavy, antique table and that no one could've moved it with their knees or any device. Danielle's friends, who had been helping earlier with the event, were later spending the night on the parlor floor. In the middle of the night, the floorboards started rattling, whether from the winds or something else. They grabbed their belongings, ran out and never returned to the house. Our volunteer, Ruthe, tells of the same Halloween event when a lamp in the parlor tilted about forty-five degrees and then righted itself.

Peyton Townsend, former Ferry director of the summer camp and junior docent, described a Friday Night Fright event when he was a teenager. He and other junior volunteers were in the Best Parlor. An old clock that hadn't worked in years sat on the fireplace mantel. Peyton described how they were standing around talking when, all of a sudden, that clock chimed on the hour. He said it continued to chime on the hour not only for the rest of the evening but also for weeks afterward. Peyton said that he had never known that clock to work. No one had touched it. No one had wound it up. He went on to describe how the group left the parlor after the clock struck, and when they walked into the hallway, they saw that every picture had been turned at an angle. Each one now hung crooked on the wall. He had no explanation but said it happened the same time that the clock had chimed.

Peyton shared another experience about a time when he and some other volunteers were upstairs and one of his friends started feeling sick. This particular person was a skeptic and not a full believer in the paranormal. However, believers and skeptics alike are vulnerable to bouts of nausea in the house. Peyton went downstairs to get her some water from the kitchen. As he was walking from the dining room into the courthouse, something stopped

Volunteer Joshua Ross during a Fright Night Fright event. *Author's collection.*

him. He felt like he couldn't step into the courthouse. He described the feeling as "so heavy" and that it was "hard to cross." Finally, he realized that he needed to get his friend some water, so he pushed through and was able to make it to the kitchen. He had no explanation for what stopped him or for what reason.

Another former volunteer told me of an experience that happened when he was a junior docent at the house. Belinda was coming down the second-floor stairs with an armful of costumes. She lost her balance and, not being able to grab the handrail, she started to fall. He remembered seeing her body stop, as if unseen arms held her and kept her from falling. She righted herself, and when she reached the bottom of the steps, there was a handprint on the front of her sweater.

One of the earlier paranormal claims we have is that of a spirit cat—maybe two. Affectionately nicknamed "Whiskers" by the volunteers, he is described as a tabby, whereas others claim that he's all black, thus leading to the theory that there are two. In the video I mentioned earlier, one of the docents tells the story of giving a tour one day, and when the group was in the dining room, a black cat walked in. They thought it had come in from outside. She described how it rubbed its back up against the wall, meowed, did a little turn and then walked straight through the wall. Her tour group quickly left. In the video, another volunteer explains that during a Halloween event, she knelt down in the parlor to get something and felt a cat rub her leg and throw its body into her. She said it was so strong and so sudden that she jumped across the room. Cody does not like cats, and often when giving history tours, the cat will rub against his leg. He tries to subtly shake his leg to make it go away but without making the guests think something is wrong with him.

Joshua Husak tells the story about a Friday Night Fright event when Cody was telling the guests about the spirit cat. Joshua, our skeptic, said he was thinking to himself, "This is stupid. There is no ghost cat." So, without Cody knowing, Joshua took a laser pointer and put the beam on the back of Cody's calf. He said Cody jumped about a foot in the air and yelled, "That was the cat!" He didn't know that Joshua had put the laser on him, causing the cat to grab it. More recently, Joshua was at the house with Cody, and while they were talking in the dining room, they both heard a very distinctive "meow." Joshua asked Cody if that was his phone, and Cody said, "You heard the cat, didn't you?" With Joshua being a skeptic, he doesn't readily believe what he experiences is paranormal. However, he said that in this case, it was clear as day. There was no question he heard a cat.

The cat also made an appearance on the recording of a board meeting. Halfway through there is an inexplicable "meow," one that was obviously not made by any board member. I have actually had several personal experiences with the cat. The first time was during our Charles Dickens performance of *A Christmas Carol*, which we used to perform at the house in December. We were between shows, and I was sitting in the library with another volunteer. While we were talking, I felt this humming feeling on the back of my leg. It felt like my phone when it's set on vibration mode. But my phone was not near my calf. It slowly lessened and faded away. After the moment passed, I realized that it must have been the cat, and he was purring as he rubbed against my leg. I had a similar experience years later when I was fixing the covering on an upstairs bed. I was leaning over and felt something on the back of my leg and assumed that I had accidentally pulled the quilt down. But when I stood up, the quilt was lying flat on the bed. On other occasions, I have heard the cat, once in the parlor, and once in my car when I was in the drive-thru line at a fast-food restaurant right after leaving Ferry.

In 2013, the paranormal show *Oddity Files* filmed an episode at Ferry Plantation. Activity started almost immediately when, just minutes after setting up their equipment, they caught an EVP of a child's voice saying, "Here we go." Throughout the night, they experienced children's voices both singing and speaking, orbs, taps on the shoulder, thuds in the nursery, a little girl peeking around the corner and the camera turning itself on and off. One of the most unusual occurrences during their visit was a glowing ball of light that traveled outside of the gift shop's window. Being too high to have been a car headlight, it was never explained.

In 2015, Ferry Plantation House made its debut on the Travel Channel in an episode of *Mysteries at the Museum*. Belinda appeared in the episode, telling the story of Grace Sherwood through the artifact of a witch ball. This episode brought widespread public awareness to the Ferry Plantation

House. In fact, this is how I became aware of the house and what made me interested in coming out for a tour. If you're interested in seeing this segment, the episode is titled "The Birth of the Road Map."

Thanks to Belinda and Herb Nash, Gerry Richter, Danielle Sheets, Donovan Lenaghan, Ann and Al Henley, Ruthe and countless others, Ferry Plantation House is fully restored from years of fundraising and hard work. Throughout the house, we have pictures of what the rooms looked like before the house was renovated. The transformation is incredible. To this day, Ferry is run 100 percent by volunteers. There is neither paid staff nor paid board members. As tour guides, we often receive compliments on our passion in sharing the house and its history. We explain that we are there because we love being there, despite having busy lives and full-time jobs outside of Ferry. Whenever someone gives me a tip at the end of a tour, I always put it as a donation to the house because this allows me to keep doing what I love best: sharing Ferry Plantation House with others.

Ferry Plantation Today

The idea is simple. That even if we don't see a spirit or hear them…
we're never truly alone.
—Anthony Sabella, WTKR, when visiting Ferry Plantation in October 2017

Ferry Plantation House appears on multiple lists as one of the most haunted locations in Virginia. In 2018, *USA Today* ran an article featuring Ferry as one of its most "spirited spots." In 2021, *Travel and Leisure* magazine named Ferry Plantation as one of the "best haunted places" nationwide. The Virginia Is for Lovers website lists Ferry on its "12 Haunted Sites in Virginia with True Ghost Stories." The Colonial Ghosts website includes Ferry in its list of "Top 25 Most Haunted Places in Virginia." And the list goes on. We also seem to appear on additional lists during the Halloween season.

To date, we've had more than six hundred paranormal teams conduct overnight investigations at the house. These groups come to reportedly haunted locations searching for evidence to prove there is life after death. In essence, they collect data to support the existence of ghosts or to find other reasons for unexplained activity. In January 2020, the famous YouTube personalities Omar Gosh and Kris Star visited Ferry. Known for their paranormal vlogs, they documented their time in the house, each recording their own paranormal experiences. We have had other famous paranormal teams contact us for an investigation, but sometimes when we share our

Aerial photo of Ferry Plantation House. *Courtesy of the Friends of Ferry Plantation House.*

rules, they lose interest. We do not allow provoking, a tactic used by some investigators to purposely instigate or anger the spirits to get a reaction. We also don't allow the use of any spirit boards, like a Ouija board, that can allow unwanted spirits to enter. We additionally require that a board member stay in the house for the duration of the investigation. Our spirits are peaceful, and we are careful not to jeopardize that.

A paranormal show recently contacted us to be featured in an upcoming episode; however, when they interviewed our volunteers, they found that our spirits weren't "scary" enough. Most on-air teams look for locations where either staff is scared to work at the location or the paranormal activity has turned threatening. Neither applies to Ferry. In Anthony Sabella's 2017 news article "Unfinished Business: An In-Depth Look at the Paranormal," he wrote that Mike Ricksecker, an Ohio-based ghost hunter, said that "spirits are usually peaceful, like those inside Ferry Plantation." In the same article, they interviewed a volunteer inside Ferry. They quoted her as saying, "There's always activity here.…You never feel unsafe here. They just want to get your attention." This statement was immediately followed by something in the parlor falling to the floor behind the news crew. Clairaudient and clairsentient Sherry Baier said on her visit that "most of the ladies in the house were happy here." And Joshua Husak said, "I've never not felt safe at Ferry. No eerie presence or like something doesn't like me or want me there." This sentiment is shared across volunteers and guests alike. If there was anything negative or evil in the house, we would not be open for the public to visit.

In 2022, 13 News Now interviewed Cody about Ferry Plantation House. He explained, "It's super active, but it's also super positive. There's nothing negative here that's going to harm anybody." He explained that our spirits are not dangerous and described the young spirit of Bessie as his hug when he arrives. He greets the house as he enters and then feels a hug around his thighs. He said, "Just because it's paranormal doesn't mean it's scary. You know, people come in here expecting to be scared because it's a haunted house. That's not how it works. They aren't always there to scare you."

In Connor Worley's news article on "Haunted Hampton Roads: The Ghosts of Ferry Plantation House," Cody shared the story of a skeptic turned believer during one of his tours. A reluctant navy man had come to the house with his girlfriend for a ghost tour. Cody could tell that he wasn't interested in being there and didn't believe the house was haunted. Suddenly the guy raised his arm and walked out of the room. Cody asked what he was doing, and he said he had no idea. He said something grabbed his hand

and was pulling him through the house. It's interesting that he stopped in front of Cody's son, who was sitting at a table playing a game on his tablet. Apparently, the little spirit, who he thinks was Bessie, was distracted by watching the game.

VOLUNTEER STORIES

I sat down with our volunteers in preparation for this book, and they each shared their experiences with me. Cody first came to the house as a paranormal investigator. He told me about his first night at the house. They were wrapping up their investigation, and Cody had gone into the parlor to start breaking down the equipment. He described how he got a blast of air right in his chest that made him sit down. He told the spirits that it was late, and he needed to pack up to go. He grabbed his equipment and went up to the conference room, where it happened again. He said the shot of air was so strong that it knocked him into a chair. He asked if they were keeping him there for a reason. He then noticed that it had started raining. He had an ovilus, a paranormal device that displays and/or speaks words from the spirits. The ovilus was still on, and it said, "Basketball." There is a basketball hoop on the tennis court. He asked if that is what they were talking about. The ovilus said, "Mischief." He asked if he should go out to the tennis court. The ovilus indicated yes.

Cody and his fellow investigator went downstairs, and when they opened the door to go out, it stopped raining. He asked if they had made it rain earlier so he wouldn't leave, but now had made it stop raining so he could go do what they asked him to do. He received the response, "Elemental." As they started walking toward the tennis court, they heard a loud muffler on a car racing down the road. This was around 4:00 a.m. and not normal for this neighborhood. They walked over to the hanging tree and found bottles of alcohol. Apparently, they had scared off a group that was hanging out and potentially getting ready to do something they shouldn't. The other investigator explained that earlier there was a similar car in the Ferry parking lot, and when they were approached, the teens gave him attitude. Cody is convinced that this group was going to do something potentially dangerous or damaging to the house or neighborhood, but the spirits alerted him and he was able to chase them off. At Ferry, we have a collective feeling that our spirits protect the house. This is the perfect example.

Ferry Plantation House at night. *Author's collection.*

Another volunteer, Ruthe, told me how one time a volunteer lay down on the sofa in the Best Parlor. She then saw a shadow figure act as if it was trying to get her attention. When she stood up to see what was going on, she saw people coming up the walkway and realized that they let her know someone was coming. She also described a time when she and Danielle, Belinda's daughter, were talking after Ruthe took part in a paranormal investigation at St. Albans Sanitorium, a notoriously haunted site in Radford, Virginia. Ruthe was saying how after investigating there, she would never be afraid at Ferry again. Just then, they heard a child laugh, as if they were mocking her last statement.

Joshua Husak is our resident skeptic, but even he claims that he can't explain some of the things he has experienced in the house. He shared that one time after an event, he spent the night at the house. Cody was there with his three boys. The next morning, Joshua woke up angry and asked Cody why he let his kids just run around the house all night. He said they kept him awake all night. Cody said he heard them too. Then he explained that his boys had left around 11:00 p.m. the night before, right after Joshua had gone to sleep.

Joshua talked about another occurrence that happened one night after they hosted *A Christmas Carol*. He was closing up the house and, from the second floor, turned off the third-floor hall light. He heard a voice say, "Turn that light back on!" He immediately switched it back on before he realized that no one should be upstairs. He went to check, and the rooms were empty. He figured he was just tired and hearing things, so he came back downstairs and turned the light back off. Just then, he heard a loud stomp from upstairs.

His wife asked what that sound was, and Joshua replied that it was nothing. But he stood silently for a minute to see if anything else would happen, and up above, he heard heavy footsteps walking across the floor.

As for our spirits, Joshua said, "They loved the house, and they're still there. They are past residents who just decided to stay around." He said that often when he's alone in the house, he feels like someone is there with him. He'll see things out of the corner of his eye. He'll walk into a room and recognize that an object is out of place. One of his most common experiences is walking into the house and finding the heavy, wooden block from our brick oven lying halfway across the floor. Most of us can't pull it out of the brick oven on a normal day because it often gets stuck. Sometimes he comes in to find cabinets open for no reason, and not the kind that randomly open on their own. He often catches the smell of perfume, thinking that the other volunteers have put out potpourri, only to find they haven't. (We've come to learn that the smell of perfume usually means that Belinda's spirit is there.) He'll find lights that have come on and will hear people walking around, especially in the parlor. Our squeaky floors let us know when someone is moving around. But when he checks, no one is there.

Joshua will sometimes have people on a history tour who will see someone in a period costume in another room, or some claim to have been touched. (During our history tours, we normally don't talk about our spirits.) He said:

> *I've been at Ferry for so many years that I now ignore a lot of things that happen. It's normal for me. For first time visitors, they would see it as not normal and ask what just happened. Like when the chandelier shakes, the people will look and ask if people are upstairs. I'm like, "No, it's just us...It shouldn't be shaking like that but it does." They ask if I'm okay with that, and I say I'm so used to it now that I don't chalk it up to paranormal—I just chalk it up to being Ferry.*

Gerry Richter has been with the house longer than anyone. She was instrumental in helping to save the house and then spent innumerable hours working alongside Belinda in its day-to-day restoration spanning over twenty years. If there is a chip in a door, she can tell you where it came from. Her knowledge and experience in the house are priceless. She often tells me tidbits of information, and I immediately write them down so we can preserve as much information as we can. (She once told me not to lick the library fireplace because there is lead in the paint.) I consider that Ferry

Children and pets sometimes refuse to go up the second-floor stairs. *Author's collection.*

has two histories: its "older" history of the land and families since the mid-1600s and then the history of the restoration. Each has its own story to tell.

As for the spirits in the house, Gerry said, "I feel no ghosts. I feel no spirits….Maybe because I was here since the beginning when this place was in shambles….I feel nothing, and I'm perfectly happy with that." As for Belinda, who was her close friend, she said that she feels she is in the house and feels that she's around us, but she doesn't sense her. Even if she doesn't pick up on the spirits in the house, she tells how her little two-pound dog does. She described a recent event when her dog went upstairs, but when it was time to go, he refused to come back down the steps. He ran and hid under one of the beds. Cindy, another volunteer, had to go up to get him. Normally, he runs carefree up and down those same stairs. Gerry told me when she and Belinda would come to work on the house in the mid-1990s, they would bring their dogs. Someone had donated cradles that were kept on the second floor. Gerry said they would come into the house, run upstairs and jump in the cradles. "They were worthless at helping," she said. "But once in a while, they would both start up the stairs and then cry and run back down and wouldn't go back up there the rest of the day….Then they were fine the next time." When mentioning the spirits while Belinda was still living, Gerry said, "She talked to them." Belinda's son, Donovan Lenaghan, added, "All the time."

Gerry, who claims to have never experienced anything paranormal at the house, had a very unusual incident recently. She had been in the house giving tours, and at closing time, she picked up her key and headed for the door. As she walked, she watched with her own eyes as the key in her hand completely and inexplicably bent in half. Ann was beside her and witnessed the whole incident. I had to laugh when she called me that night to tell me what happened. She said things like that just don't happen to her. We teased her, saying that the spirits were tired of her not acknowledging them.

Ann Henley, another long-term volunteer, has dedicated many years to Ferry Plantation House. She was instrumental in those earlier fundraiser events. She and her husband, Al, are a wealth of knowledge on early Princess Anne County, especially around the Pungo area, where they have lived all their lives. She is one of the hardest workers I know. She's always ready and willing to take on any task that needs to be done at Ferry, whether it is painting, changing air filters, cleaning, placing personalized bricks in our walkway, sewing colonial clothes and so on. Her specialty, however, is gardening. She keeps our colonial gardens beautiful through her knowledge of plants and is always willing to share her fig jam that she makes from the fig tree in front of the house. While Ann doesn't feel any spirits at the house, she shared several unexplained occurrences.

Ann explained how Belinda used to have the Girl Scouts come out to earn a badge in colonial history. They would often spend the night (not for anything paranormal). One night, she said there were about fifteen girls and a few mothers in the conference room. They were all stretched out, ready for the night. One girl, who had been rather picky, said, "I told you I didn't want anyone sitting on my sleeping bag!" Ann said you could clearly see the imprint where someone had been sitting. It was around midnight, everyone was tired, and Belinda told her that no one had been sitting there. When the girl slid into her sleeping bag and kicked that spot, a dog barked. They all heard it. But there was no dog in the room, nor had there been one at any time that night. It seems the spirit dog had created the impression on her sleeping bag. Ann said about ten of the girls then called their parents to come pick them up!

Ann also told the story about the day her granddaughter and her friend came to Ferry to hang out while Ann was giving tours. While the girls were up in the conference room, they were expecting something to happen because they had heard the stories, but it was quiet. Finally, Ann's granddaughter said, "If there is a spirit here, I want you to pull the redhead girl's hair." They both had red hair, but Ann's granddaughter's was much brighter. Nothing happened, so they decided to go downstairs. Just then, a gush of air went past her granddaughter and pulled her hair out of her ponytail. She ran down the steps and told her friend to stop pushing her. When she stopped to look, her friend was still at the top of the stairs. When she got to the bottom, her back was itching, so they pulled up the back of her shirt and she had a red mark down the center of her back and across her waist, like someone had scratched her. They ran outside to tell Ann and haven't been back since.

Ann ended by talking about an incident that happened one night during a board meeting. The meeting was held one winter evening, and they all had a key and locked the door as they came in. Donovan was late, and they were waiting on him to start. Finally, they heard this *clump*, *clump*, *clump* coming up the stairs, but Donovan never came into the conference room. They got up to look, and no one was there. About a minute later, Donovan called to say that he couldn't make the meeting. So they all split up—half went upstairs and half went downstairs—to make sure nobody was in the house. There aren't many places to hide, so they quickly concluded that no one was there. They began the meeting, and one of the board member's chairs rolled on its own up to the table. She looked at Gerry and asked why she pushed her chair, but Gerry told her she hadn't. She was busy taking minutes. Ann said that the temperature then dropped about twenty degrees. Everyone looked at one another and agreed that the meeting was over. They went downstairs, and a lamp in the library started turning on and off. They thought Ann was doing it, but she wasn't anywhere near the switch. They checked the house once more, turned off the lights, locked up and were soon walking down the sidewalk. Someone dropped something, and when they did, they looked back to the house and saw that two lights had come back on. Ann looked at Gerry, but neither volunteered to go back in, deciding to just turn them off the following morning when they reopened for tours.

Lights turning on at Ferry is one of the more common occurrences at the house. Each time we close, the last job is to go through the house to make sure all the lights are turned off. Many times, when we come back several days later, we'll find a light on. This mostly seems to happen on the second-story landing and in the adjacent bathroom. I know there have been many times when I have turned off lights, only to come home and check our security cameras to find one has come back on. Cody said that often after overnight investigations, he'll walk down the sidewalk to his car, turn back and will watch a light come on. Like Gerry and Ann, he leaves it until his next visit.

Cindy Core shared that one day, she and Cathy Hunt were in the gift shop, talking about Cathy's recent trip to Nova Scotia. Cathy was sharing how she knew Belinda was from Canada, and she felt her presence on that vacation. While they were talking, Cindy felt someone put a hand on her shoulder. She turned around, but no one was there. She said that was the first time she'd felt anything "human like" touch her in the house. I actually had a

Ferry Plantation House under a full moon. *Author's collection.*

very similar experience. I was in the conference room looking through photo albums from the early 2000s. I saw a picture of Gerry, Ann and Belinda all together for a Ferry event. I put my hand on the picture because I could feel their friendship and their love for Ferry through this particular picture. It was an "awww" type of moment, and I may have even said that out loud. Just then, I felt a hand on my head. I could feel the gentle, slight weight, and a tingling sensation ran across my scalp. I remember shuddering, and then it was gone. As I recounted this later, Cindy said, "That's what I felt too. It was comforting. Like something a mom would do."

Cathy went on to describe an experience she had in the dining room. She was looking at the mourning dress that we have on display, and while she was touching it, it started to shake all over. She was afraid it was going to fall over. She drew back her hand and said, "Okay, I'm done. I'll leave you alone," and it went right back into its place. Even after an experience like this, Cathy said, "I just feel comfort in this house." She first came to the house with her son for a Friday Night Fright event and, afterward, asked how she could volunteer. When she got into the car to leave that night, she noticed the clock in her car had stopped at the time when they first arrived. They pushed all kinds of buttons, but it wouldn't change back to regular time. The day she came back to volunteer, she talked with Cody for a while, and when she left, the clock went right back to the correct time. She said to herself, "I'm meant to be here."

Cathy continued by saying, "I don't feel anything bad...when I go up there [to the nanny's room], I say, 'Hey, Nanny. I love you to death, but I'm just here to clean.' I've never had any experiences in there, even cleaning the room. It doesn't bother me." Cindy immediately chimed in, saying:

> *She unplugged my vacuum! I was in the hallway. I had done the nanny's room and went to vacuum the wood, and then suddenly the vacuum cuts off. I got that feeling and was afraid to turn around, but I've got to do this. I'm up here by myself, so I turned around, went back into that room. That cord didn't fall. It was yanked and was laying a good six inches from the outlet. I told her, "I'm sorry, I know it's loud, but I need to finish" and then got out of there.*

Donovan's wife, Margaret, said, "You know how much history has happened here, but I don't feel like a presence, but I'm very aware of how much has happened in this house." She and Donovan both brought up the idea of power of suggestion, especially with some of the children who grew up hearing the stories. Margaret said, "Some of the young ones in our family were told this happened to you, but then there are other kids who would have no way of being influenced....I believe they are here, I just haven't experienced it...but I'm okay with them not wanting to interact with me. I've never felt uncomfortable or nervous in this house....Maybe they're not always aware of us or maybe they aren't here all the time. We don't know how it works."

On a separate occasion, Donovan and Margaret's daughter, Lauren, shared an experience that she had as a child. She was attending the summer history camp that Ferry used to host, and she and her friend were coming down the second-story stairs. About halfway down, her T-shirt suddenly pulled out in front of her, like someone had grabbed it. She looked at her friend, and the back of her T-shirt was doing the same thing. It was as if someone was standing in between the two girls, pulling on both of their shirts. She said it then let go, and both girls raced the rest of the way down the steps.

PARANORMAL TEAMS

Ferry Plantation House has been investigated more than six hundred times by paranormal groups. I can't think of a time that a group walked away without any evidence. Some nights are more active than others, but it's rare that our spirits don't show up at all.

In March 2024, Old Dominion Ghost Hunters investigated the house. When they first arrived, one of their team members went into the downstairs bathroom. Ruthe and I were at the dining room table in the next room. He came out and asked if we had knocked on the door. We said no. He said that someone knocked while he was in there, and he even said he would be out in a minute. The team hadn't even set up their equipment yet, and there was already activity. Later in the evening, they were in the nanny's room and heard a loud noise in the corner. They tilted up a rocking chair and saw a smiley face drawn in the dust on the floor. They asked, "Did you draw the smiley face?" and they heard a voice with their own ears say, "Yes." I went up to see it for myself, and it was in the very back corner of the room in an area not easily reached. It wasn't a typical smiley face, but one that looked like it was drawn with two fingers instead of just one. But it was a smiley face nonetheless. During the rest of the evening, the team experienced drained

Smiley face found by paranormal investigators in the dust on the floor of the nanny's room. *Author's collection.*

batteries and heard voices, a woman humming and footsteps on the nanny's stairs. At one point, the door to the nursery closet opened by itself. All in all, a fairly typical investigation at Ferry Plantation House.

OTHER ACCOUNTS

A psychic medium with a paranormal group once told me that she could feel the different periods of time as she walked from one end of the house to the other. That makes sense because Ferry was built in three sections from the 1700s through the mid-1800s. I expressed my frustration to this same woman that I have never seen any of our spirits. She explained that they don't show themselves to me because I already know they're there. They don't have to prove themselves.

On the sofa in the Best Parlor, we have two pictures from paranormal investigations. One we believe to be the spirit of Isabella McIntosh as she continues to wait for her husband, Charles, to come back from war. It clearly shows the reflection of a pregnant woman with brown hair, wearing a blue dress, looking down while standing by the parlor window. The other is of a young blond girl reflected in the front window of the Green Room. She seems to be wearing a faded pink dress with a white pinafore or apron. Her hair is pulled into two braids. There is some discrepancy as to who she might be. Some think she might be Sally Rebecca Walke, while others say it could be Bessie. Several of the mediums visiting the house claim to see blond children. Ambrosia saw a little blond girl around ten years old in the hall, and she picked up the name Ann. While we're not sure who this girl is, we do know that she decided to make herself known to the paranormal team that evening.

We have several early accounts of a woman's spirit in white riding a penny farthing–style bicycle, where the front wheel is much larger than the one in back. She had been seen by multiple people, including several guests in attendance at an oyster roast held at Ferry. A friend had asked Belinda to introduce him to her at the end of an event. Not knowing who he was referring to, she soon forgot. He continued to see her two more times that night and ended up leaving heartbroken that he was never introduced. Belinda realized later that this woman could not have been of our world and explained this to her friend, so he wouldn't continue to pine away for someone he could never meet.

SPIRITS OF THE GIFT SHOP/OLDER GIRLS' ROOM

The gift shop used to be the older girls' room in the nineteenth century. It's one of my favorite rooms because it's very bright, and when the sun comes in through the window behind the stand of witch balls, the room dances with color. The beige wallpaper above the crown molding and the dusty pink color below give the room a welcoming feeling.

As I mentioned earlier, Eric seems to be most active in this room. We believe it is he who knocks tins of tea off the shelf but is generally seen as a happy but mischievous little boy. Luckily, his antics are limited to tins of tea instead of breaking any of our numerous glass witch balls that hang in the windows. We also believe that he is the one who opens cabinet doors in this room. Recently, Celtic Protection Paranormal was investigating the house, and during their tour, I explained about the cabinet doors opening in that room. They firmly closed the higher cubby doors and made sure that the closet door was securely shut. They then left to investigate elsewhere in the house. When they returned to the room hours later, they found both cubby doors and the closet door wide open. They then put a camera facing that side of the room, but the doors didn't open again that night. It was just as well since the camera they set up inexplicably turned itself off after they left the room.

Cousins from the Hudgins/Howren families said that when they visited Ferry, they would sleep in this room. At night, they would see a woman pacing across the floor in front of the fireplace. When Sherry Baier of 7 Cities Paranormal visited in 2013, she saw a young girl in a long white dressing gown with elaborate lace on the sleeves and bodice. She gave the impression of being very prissy and always wore lace. Sherry picked up that she loved to ride horses and would sneak down to the river to swim. She seemed to be very demanding, inheriting this trait from her mother. She had this particular room to herself. She was expected to marry well and expected only the very best. Sherry sensed that she was very smart. Was this perhaps Charles McIntosh's daughter, Anne "Nannie" Dornin, who would later marry a successful doctor?

Peyton Townsend shared an event that also took place in this room. Serving as Ferry's director of the summer camp, Peyton explained how they never talked to the campers about the spirits or told them any ghost stories. Summer camp was focused only on early American history and way of life. One day, a family came for a tour during summer camp, and they were looking around the gift shop. Peyton said they had a little boy about six years

The cubby and closet doors in the gift shop opened on their own during a paranormal investigation. *Author's collection.*

old who kept talking to himself in the corner. Peyton went over to him and asked who he was talking to. The little boy responded that he was talking to Henry and had been this whole time. No one on the tour or from summer camp had mentioned Henry to the family. Peyton also shared that during summer camp, he often heard little feet running up and down the third-floor stairs at times before the children arrived or while the campers were in the conference room.

SPIRITS OF THE LIBRARY

The Ferry volunteers often associate the spirit of Stella Barnett with the library. However, other spirits have been felt there as well. When Sherry visited, she saw two women working on a bedspread that was stretched across a large hoop. One woman was very afraid of the fire. She was worried the rug near the fireplace would catch fire. Ten years later in the same room, another psychic medium said she was pushed back from the fireplace and told not to get too close because she could get burned. Recently, a third medium visiting Ferry also sensed that there was a woman keeping her back away from the fireplace.

When I spend the night at Ferry for overnight investigations, I usually sleep in the library. One night, I was with Ruthe, and we both got settled on the floor to go to sleep. Just as I started to drift off, I very clearly heard a woman call my name. I sat up, thinking that Ruthe had gotten up and needed something. But when I looked over, Ruthe was asleep on the floor. I looked into the dining room, where I heard the voice come from. No one was there. I later shared this with Gerry and Ann, and they told me that all the women in the house know me, so it wouldn't be unusual for one of them to call my name.

BREEZEWAY SPIRITS

The central hallway, or breezeway, in the middle of the house is often perceived to be the busiest as far as spirit activity. Some mediums have seen people waiting in chairs, which would have been typical in colonial times, as guests would first wait in the hall before being invited into the office,

The breezeway is believed to be busy with spirit activity. *Author's collection.*

library or parlor by the host. One medium believed that at one time the hall was wider to accommodate the many waiting visitors. Sherry Baier shared that she felt that both the landside and waterside doors were often open at the same time to allow for a good cross breeze. She was told that on more than one occasion a gust of wind would slam both doors closed, scaring everyone in the house. Even though there is a deadbolt and alarm now on both doors, we have come in numerous times to find these doors unlocked. This is unusual since we rarely use these doors, preferring the side entry instead. I opened one day for tours to find the front door completely swung open. Perhaps the spirits were still looking for that wonderful cross breeze.

Children's spirits have often been seen sitting on the hall steps that lead up to the second floor. I was once told by a young sensitive girl not to step on the children as I walked up the steps. There was one time when I was in the dining room, and I heard a very loud tapping from the hall, sounding like someone tapping a pen against the glass in one of the pictures. I had to go upstairs, crossing through the hall. I didn't see anything out of place but continued up the steps. I had just been working outside raking up magnolia leaves and was exhausted. When I reached the top of the stairs, I heard a loud sigh right beside me. Instead of being scared, I thought, "Why are *you* tired and sighing when I've been the one outside working all day?"

Belinda's cloak still hangs in the hallway, and there is a picture of her on the wall. During my tours, I stop in the breezeway and talk about her. I tell who she was, how she helped save the house, all the hard work she did to restore the home, her fundraising events and so on. On more than one tour, before even mentioning Belinda, I've had guests ask me where the smell of perfume is coming from. Whiffs of perfume are associated with Belinda, especially with people who knew her and can recognize the fragrance she used to wear. I feel she is still very much in the house and often comes with us on our tours.

BEST PARLOR SPIRITS

The Best Parlor tends to be one of the active rooms for paranormal activity in the house. We believe that since this was the social center of the house, it has held on to much of that energy. Also, it was used as the "death room" if someone passed away. An early psychic medium visiting the house felt that this room was used like a tavern or pub. He described it as a "boisterous"

Guests, volunteers and investigators have experienced a high level of paranormal activity in the Best Parlor. *Author's collection.*

room with lots of music, dancing and parties. He saw that the family would move the furniture up against the walls to give more room for dancing. He saw a pianoforte, a Chinese punch bowl (popular during the mid-1800s), a harp, a violin, mirrors and candles. Volunteers have sometimes heard a woman humming or singing, with the sound coming from the parlor.

One fall day, I was outside raking leaves, and the volunteer with me had classical music playing on his phone while we worked. We were on the waterside of the house, working outside the parlor window. While I was raking, I suddenly only heard a violin playing. I thought that was odd and not like the other music we had been listening to. When I looked up to ask him about it, I realized he was down in the parking lot, hauling a bag of leaves. I glanced around to see where the music was coming from, and when I looked into the parlor window, the music stopped. We are in a neighborhood, but the likelihood of a neighbor sitting outside playing a violin seemed unlikely. Is it possible that I caught part of a spirit performance? Or did I interrupt a dinner party still being held by the family?

On another occasion, I had pulled into the parking lot for tours, and I noticed Ann's car was already there. When I got up to the house and was passing by the first-floor windows, I heard knocking on the glass. I looked up, smiling, expecting to see Ann looking out. I didn't see her in the window beside me, so I looked to the others but couldn't find her. I looked up to the second-floor windows, but there was a glare so I couldn't see very well. I decided I would just tell her when I came in that I heard her knock but couldn't find the right window. We keep the outside door locked, so I grabbed my key, unlocked the door, walked in and immediately was alerted to turn off the alarm. I did, but then realized, if I was the first to turn off the alarm, no one else was in the house. We do have shutters that don't sit flush to the house, and they bang against the brick with every breeze. However, I know that sound, and what I heard was different. It sounded like knocking on the glass. It turned out that it wasn't Ann's car in the parking lot, just one that looked similar. Instead of being scared by the experience, I felt honored that someone had wanted to greet me as I approached the house.

This book has been challenging to finish. Each time I thought I was done writing, I would go to Ferry and come home with another story. Or another paranormal team would visit and experience new unexplained activity. Every time something happens, I look at whomever I'm with and say, "I love Ferry." You just never know what is going to happen next.

Grace Sherwood

The Witch of Pungo

Witch.... *For this was a word invented by man, a word that brings power to those who speak it, not to those it describes.*
—*Emilia Hart,* Weyward

A statue of Grace Sherwood sits at the corner of Independence Boulevard and North Witchduck Road in Virginia Beach. Colorful flowers often peek out of the bronze bag that Grace carries in one hand, while the other hand holds herbs. Local Grace Sherwood admirers keep the statue adorned with seasonal plastic flowers year-round. Grace is depicted wearing a modest laced bodice dress with a scarf tied and resting on her shoulders. Her hair is pulled back at the base of her neck and kept in place by a mop cap. A curious raccoon stands on its hind legs and rests a paw on Grace's skirt. A small, flat satchel rests against her hip. In her day, it surely held herbs that many say she collected for her remedies, for tradition claims that Grace Sherwood was a healer. According to legend, in the late 1600s and early 1700s, she served her small community of Pungo, located in eastern Princess Anne County. However, through religious convictions and superstitions of the time, she was accused of being a witch by her neighbors and unjustly earned the name the "Witch of Pungo."

A wide variety of fanciful tales have developed throughout the past three hundred years about the famed Witch of Pungo. History mixes with folklore to create the modern-day narrative of Grace Sherwood. Dr. Scott Moore has taken an in-depth look into the story of Grace in his book *The*

Witch of Pungo: Grace Sherwood in Virginia History and Legend. His research separates fact from fiction and allows us to better understand how this simple woman from rural Princess Anne County grew into a popular local legend. While Moore's book discusses the many tales told about Grace, I will share the story as we tell it at Ferry Plantation. This tale owes much to Belinda Nash, the house's early founder, who spent more than twenty years thoroughly researching the life of Grace Sherwood. She and her daughter, Danielle Sheets, compiled their work into a book, *A Place in Time: The Age of the Witch of Pungo*. Grace's story is rooted in fact but interspersed with fiction, as people throughout the years have filled in the gaps of Grace's fragmented historical record.

Statue of Grace Sherwood. *Author's collection.*

In our telling of Grace's story, she was born to John and Susan White in 1660 on Muddy Creek Road in the Pungo area of Princess Anne County. (At that time, a "road" meant a waterway.) Grace was baptized in the Christian traditions, her family being members of the 1st Lynnhaven Parish Church. Legend has it that when she was a child, her Scottish father taught her skills that most men of the time would've taught their sons—how to farm, take care of livestock, fish, navigate the creeks, work nautical knots, identify marine life and other necessary skills—as they traveled the waterways of the Chesapeake Bay and its tributaries. Her mother came from England and taught Grace a wealth of information about weather patterns, plants, trees and gardening. She also imparted her knowledge about picking, drying and preparing plants and herbs to make medicinal remedies. During this time, there were no drugstores to run to when someone had a headache. Instead, the sick person would visit the local healer, who would boil the bark from a willow tree to "rid their head of demons." In other words, they would provide the ingredients now found in modern-day aspirin to cure a headache. Grace grew up well rounded and very much in tune with the natural world. As she grew into adulthood, she used healing herbs to cure

Church Point, the location of the 1st Lynnhaven Parish Church where James and Grace Sherwood were believed to have been married in 1680. *Author's collection.*

animals, treat neighbors when they were sick and likely served as a midwife, especially after the passing of her mother.

In 1680, at the age of twenty, Grace White married James Sherwood at the 1st Lynnhaven Parish Church. (The church is no longer standing but was located at present-day Church Point, not far from the Adam Thoroughgood House.) James was a carpenter and built a home for his bride on the 50 acres of land on Muddy Creek that Grace's father had given them as a wedding gift. When her father passed away soon after, the couple received the remainder of his 145 acres. They continued to live on this land as their own family soon grew to include three sons: John, James and Richard. Together, they had a successful farm because Grace had been taught at an early age how to irrigate the earth so that in case of a bad storm or flooding, they would not lose their crops, such as tobacco, cotton, wild rice, vegetables and herbs. Her parents had also taught her how to dry wheat and grains so that they didn't mold and go to waste. Grace and James raised healthy livestock, knowing how to cure them when they fell ill and making sure that their basic needs were met, such as having access to fresh, clean water. Such ideas are common sense to us now, but back in their time, this was not common knowledge among the early colonists.

In the late 1600s, religious beliefs in Princess Anne County were shaped by the idea that if you lived as a devoted Christian and had faith, God would reward you and give you favor through prosperity. However, if you sinned and had not confessed, it was believed that God would send illness to you, your family and/or livestock. Punishment could also result in the devastation of their farms and thus their livelihood. When some of Grace's neighbors began experiencing misfortune with their crops and animals and they saw that the Sherwood farm was prospering, it was easier to place blame than perhaps admitting to their own sins or failings.

Grace Sherwood, Witch of Pungo by William George "Rip" Rylance. *Courtesy of the Friends of Ferry Plantation House.*

In 1698, jealous neighbors started claiming that their livestock were sick and their crops were failing due to Grace's involvement not with herbal remedies but with witchcraft. Some accused her of bewitching their land and animals. During this time, husbands would bring charges and represent their wives in court. On March 3, 1698, James brought their neighbor Richard Capps to court on the charge of slander against Grace. There was no specific mention of what the slander entailed, and the case was settled out of court. However, just a year and half later, on September 10, 1698, James filed another suit against their neighbors Jane and John Gisburne and Anthony and Elizabeth Barnes, also for slander against Grace. The Gisburnes had publicly claimed that Grace had bewitched their farm, causing their pigs to die and their cotton not to grow.

The story the Barneses told was a bit more fanciful. Elizabeth Barnes claimed that one night while she was sleeping, Grace Sherwood sneaked into her bedroom and rode her around the ceiling like a horse. (Witches were known to ride people like horses. Since witches were known to terrorize people at night, this is possibly where the term *nightmare* comes from.) After Grace supposedly rode Elizabeth around, she then turned herself into a black cat and slipped out through the keyhole. This is actually documented in the court records. James brought nine character witnesses to this trial, but the jury found for the defendants in both the Barnes and Gisburne cases.

Things were quiet for the next few years. In 1701, James Sherwood died, leaving Grace with their three boys to raise, along with managing the farm. In this day and age, women did not take on this kind of

House on Grace Sherwood's Land by William George "Rip" Rylance. *Courtesy of the Friends of Ferry Plantation House.*

responsibility. The expectation was that she would remarry and that her new husband would assume the responsibility of running the farm. With nearly two hundred acres and three older sons to help work the land, it would be surprising if Grace wasn't pursued by a number of suitors. She was also rumored to be of "fair face and form." However, she was fiercely independent and remained a widow for the rest of her life. This certainly was not normal, and she would have been watched very carefully by her neighbors and townspeople. Not one to worry about appearances, Grace sparked gossip in Pungo by wearing James's pants while working out in the fields. During this time, only a husband should know his wife's shape, so any female wearing pants was scandalous. The distrust and resentment from the women in town only grew stronger.

Now without a husband to represent her in court, Grace was on her own. On December 7, 1705, she brought suit against Luke and Elizabeth Hill for the charge of assault and battery. In Moore's book, he wrote that "the defendant's wife had assaulted, bruised, maimed, and barbarously beaten her." While we don't know what precipitated this, Grace asked for fifty pounds sterling for damages. This time the justices found in favor of Grace but ordered that the Hills pay only twenty shillings (about one pound, or sixty-six dollars). Moore explained that, ironically, the court paperwork was not signed, and Grace never received even that meager award. It seems a bit suspicious that all paperwork from the other trials that day was correctly signed. Even without paying the money awarded to Grace in the trial, Luke and Elizabeth Hill were not happy with the verdict. Up until now, neighbors had been able to slander Grace and spread rumors without any repercussions since Grace lost all her previous lawsuits. However, the Hills were now being held accountable, when in their eyes, it was Grace Sherwood causing all the problems. It may also be worth noting that the Hills were good friends with Anthony and Elizabeth Barnes.

Moore explained that during these times, if a woman went to court for slander, it was often due to an accusation of either sexual impropriety or a result of being outspoken, headstrong or stubborn. If Grace demonstrated a strong personality, it's understandable that there would be conflicts and disputes with her neighbors. Remaining unmarried and breaking conventional norms surely fueled the ongoing speculation that she was different, and therefore, a threat to their community. It was also during this time that "healers" were often renamed "witches" based on the current needs of the townspeople. If they were sick, they would seek out the healer. If they held a grudge or didn't approve of a woman's ways, then she was deemed a witch.

In retaliation for the court's verdict and their personal humiliation, Luke and Elizabeth Hill began publicly accusing Grace of witchcraft and formally brought charges against her. They went to court on January 3, 1706, but Grace didn't appear. On February 7, the court met and decided to summon a jury of women to search Grace's body for marks of the devil. Witches were believed to have familiars, or spirits in the form of animals (often dogs, cats, frogs or owls), that would do their bidding and aid in casting their evil spells. Familiars craved blood, so as a reward for their work, they would suckle from the witch's teat or mark. A devil's mark, or witch's mark, could be a skin tag, mole, birthmark, scar or any imperfection of the skin. If this was their basis for determining a witch, just about anyone could be accused. However, this was the belief of the time, so in his book *Witchcraft in Colonial Virginia*, Carson Hudson described a jury of "ancient and knowing women" who searched Grace's body on March 7, 1706. They found two marks that they claimed were like teats and could never be found on another woman's body. The bias was blatant, as Elizabeth Barnes served as the forewoman for this jury.

Witch balls, believed to protect a home by capturing evil spirits, hang in the windows at Ferry Plantation House. *Author's collection.*

The Hills felt that their case was not progressing as quickly as they wanted in the Princess Anne County court, so later that March, they took their complaint to the attorney general in Williamsburg. The justices there heard their case but said that the accusation was too general and that the Princess Anne County court needed to investigate further. If they found compelling evidence, they could return.

The case continued in Princess Anne County in May and June 1706. Tradition says that the justices told Grace that if she confessed her sins in front of the church, they would dismiss the charges. They supposedly stood Grace in front of the congregation, where she loudly proclaimed, "I be not a witch, I be a healer." As a result, the justices had no choice but to continue investigating the charges. The sheriff sent a group of men to search Grace's house for suspicious items that could be used for witchcraft. None was found.

It is likely that they also searched for objects that could be used to protect from witchcraft such as a witch bottle, witch ball or horseshoe. During colonial times, when a new home was built, the custom was to fill a small vial with iron nails, brass pins and urine. It was to be placed upside down under either the front porch or the hearth. The urine would allegedly attract evil spirits. They would enter the bottle and be shredded by the sharp objects, thus protecting the family.

The practice of using a witch ball came from an old English custom of hanging beveled glass balls in the windows of the home. Each ball had strands of glass or webbing inside. The crackled glass would attract any ill-meaning spirits and catch them in the webbing inside the ball. This is where we get the expression "don't let the ball drop," as you wouldn't want to release any evil you had captured.

Above: Replica witch bottle at Ferry Plantation. Witch bottles were used in colonial America to protect against evil spells and curses. *Author's collection.*

Opposite: Bells were placed on doors in colonial homes to protect against witches. Bells can be seen hanging on door knobs throughout Ferry Plantation House. *Author's collection.*

Those suspecting someone of witchcraft would have also looked for a horseshoe in the home. Even though witches were known to ride people around like horses, they were supposedly scared of horses. Therefore, if you were to hang a horseshoe above your door, it was believed to keep the witches away. Of course, this later became used as a symbol of good luck.

Grace Sherwood was not a woman prone to superstitious beliefs, so she did not have any of these protections in her house. According to her accusers, who would not have such items in their home? Why, a witch of course!

On June 7, 1706, another jury of women was summoned by the court to search Grace again for witch's marks. No one showed. It is unclear whether the women believed in Grace's innocence or truly thought she was a witch and feared retaliation in the form of curses. The case was continued until the next court day, July 5. However, when that day arrived, they were still unable to gather a jury of women to search Grace's body. It was then decided, with Grace's agreement, to give her a trial by water, also known as a "witch ducking." In their book, Nash and Sheets wrote that she was to be thrown into the Lynnhaven River "above a man's depth" to determine if she was a witch. The understanding was that if she floated, the purity of the water had rejected her, and she was guilty of being a witch. If the pure water accepted her, she was pulled to the bottom of the river and drowned, but she was innocent and could be buried on church property. In her book *Gateway to the New World*, Florence Kimberly Turner wrote that, ironically, a terrible storm came up that day, and the court decided to delay the ducking of Grace until July 10 so as to not "endanger her health."

On July 10, 1706, at ten o'clock in the morning, Grace was put in a cart at the second Princess Anne County courthouse and taken down what is now known as Witchduck Road. (This courthouse stood where Old Donation Church now stands on North Witchduck Road.) She was taken to John Harper's Plantation, which is now known as Witchduck Point. When Grace reached the shore of the Lynnhaven River, hordes of townspeople lined the bank. There had never been a witchducking in Virginia, and spectators came out in droves to witness this unprecedented event.

According to legend, as Grace was loaded into the waiting boat, it is said that she turned to the crowd lined up on the shore and declared, "Before this day be through you will all receive a worse ducking than me!" They proceeded to seat Grace and rowed out two hundred yards to the deepest part of the Lynnhaven River. There, a group of women checked her to make sure she didn't have anything on her to assist her. Then they proceeded to cross-bind her. This means they tied her right thumb to her left big toe and tied her left thumb to her right big toe. Then they threw her overboard…and she immediately rose to the surface. The pure water had rejected her, proving that she was a witch! They pulled her back into the boat. Deciding to give her a second chance, they cross-bound her again, but this time, the story goes, they placed a thirteen-pound Bible around her neck for good measure. They threw her over again…and she came right back up. Not only was she freed from her restraints, but she swam around the boat and laughed at them. (Remember that Grace's father had taught her how to swim and how to work nautical knots.)

Grace was pulled back into the boat and rowed ashore. Legend has it that just as they reached the bank where all the townspeople were cheering and jeering, a terrible storm came up. Lightning and thunder dominated the skies, and torrential rain fell. So much water fell in such a short period of time that the river flooded and washed townspeople, carts and horses out into the river. Grace had warned them. This confirmed their belief that she

Left: Ann Henley, Honorary Witch of Pungo, at the Pungo Strawberry Festival in 2001. *Courtesy of the Friends of Ferry Plantation House.*

Opposite: Belinda Nash successfully advocated to restore the good name of Grace Sherwood in 2006. *Courtesy of the Friends of Ferry Plantation House.*

had caused the storm and was indeed a witch. As a child, Grace's mother had taught her about nature, so she would've noticed the leaves curling right before a storm. Plus, anyone in Virginia knows that on a hot July day, a storm can arise out of nowhere.

Grace was taken back to the courthouse, and that's where her story is put on pause until she was given her land back in 1714. We do not know exactly what happened. She may have been locked up in jail for the next seven years. Perhaps the case was taken once more to Williamsburg, where it could have been dismissed, or Grace could have been convicted. Maybe there was a minor punishment from the local court, and she then was released. Or it's possible that she was held as a servant and served out her sentence in someone's home. No court records remain to tell us what

happened. Unfortunately, many records that could have told us the ending to the story were destroyed during the Civil War. We do know, however, that seven years later, Grace Sherwood was given back her land and lived out the rest of her years quietly on her farm on Muddy Creek Road in Pungo. She died in 1740 at the age of eighty when life expectancy at that time was thirty-seven years.

Over the years, local tradition has not only incorporated details into the scant historical records left behind, but many legends and folklore about Grace Sherwood have also grown up around Virginia Beach. The most well known collection of these folk stories come from Louisa Venable Kyle's book *The Witch of Pungo*. In it, Kyle tells the story of how Grace wanted rosemary for a dish she was preparing, but Virginia didn't have any. So she sailed back to England in an eggshell to get some. Since then, rosemary has flourished and grows all throughout Virginia Beach, even at Ferry Plantation.

Here is also a popular story about Grace's burial. Many say that when she died, her sons buried her in Pungo, and the next day, they woke up to find the coffin sitting on top of the ground. Pungo is a marshy area, so this was marginally possible after a heavy rain. Legend says that they reburied her, this time putting heavy stones on top of the coffin. The next day, they came out to find the coffin sitting once again on top of the ground, but this time, a black cat was sitting on top. Neighbors and townspeople were convinced that Grace Sherwood had come back as a cat. Sadly, it is said that they killed as many cats as they could in Princess Anne County to keep Grace away. It's historically recorded that Princess Anne County had the worst infestation of mice and other rodents that year.

When Belinda Nash began looking into local history as it pertained to Ferry Plantation, she started finding information on Grace Sherwood. She began her own research to find out who this woman was and what happened to her. She soon had a mission to tell Grace's story and to advocate for her as a healer, not as a witch. Belinda soon began petitioning the Virginia governor, asking him to pardon Grace Sherwood. She wrote to several governors over the years, and finally on July 10, 2006, Governor Tim Kaine

Local street names still reflect the 1706 ducking of Grace Sherwood. Witchduck Road is now a popular thoroughfare in Virginia Beach. *Author's collection.*

officially restored the good name of Grace Sherwood, three hundred years to the day and time that she was tried by water.

Soon after, Belinda started fundraising for a statue of Grace Sherwood. Once the statue was ready, there was much discussion and disagreement as to where it should be placed. All these years later, the Witch of Pungo still created controversy. It was finally decided that the statue would be placed in front of Sentara Independence Hospital. It was the perfect location since Grace was a healer. Ironically, she stands only a few hundred feet from where the courthouse once stood where she was originally tried and condemned by her community.

The banks of the Lynnhaven River at Witchduck Bay are now privately owned, so it's impossible to get close to the river to see the view that Grace would have seen that July day in 1706. Of course, more than three hundred years of erosion and land development have greatly altered the landscape. For several years, Ferry Plantation hosted reenactments of Grace's ducking. Belinda said this of the first reenactment on July 10, 2002:

> *Upon arriving at the pre-marked spot and gazing at the shore where Grace herself had once the same water view, the adrenaline flow was incredible. I pictured the hundreds of people lining the shore chanting, "Duck the Witch! Duck the Witch!" As I have devoted so many years of research to fully understand what Grace Sherwood had gone through, this was the most incredible experience for me.*

THE SPIRIT OF GRACE SHERWOOD

For as many legends exist regarding Grace Sherwood, there are just as many stories from those who claim to have seen her spirit. The most popular stories seem to occur around the site of her ducking on the Lynnhaven River. Many claim to feel Grace's restless spirit along the water. Residents in this area of Witchduck Bay report seeing strange lights every July on the anniversary of her trial by water. Some also claim to see a woman with long wet hair walking along the river at night. Others believe that if you lean into the wind at the site of her ducking, you can hear the jeers from the crowd and Grace's laughter. Other locals claim that if you look out over the surface of the Lynnhaven River, you can see Grace peer out of the water with a saddened expression.

Despite popular belief and numerous references on the internet, Grace Sherwood is not buried at Ferry Plantation. Like most Virginians at the time, she was most likely buried on her farm in Pungo. Belinda tells us that she's in hallowed ground where the "grass will not grow and the snow will not lie." Ivy supposedly covers her grave. But for those who believe that Grace was truly a witch, they claim that nothing will grow on her grave because this is where Grace danced with the devil. This also correlates with the local folklore that says that Virginia Beach doesn't have fireflies—just the flicker of Grace's lantern as she dances with the devil. Another legend says that Grace was buried under a tree on her property. Every full moon, feral cats gather, climb the tree and howl. It is said that Grace's spirit rises and joins them.

Not only is Grace Sherwood not buried at Ferry Plantation, but she was also never jailed there. The courthouse section of the house wasn't built until 1735, almost thirty years after her trial by water. However, there are stories of Grace's spirit appearing at Ferry. An older Virginia Beach resident recalls playing at the house back in the 1910s and 1920s. She would see servants run out of the house, claiming to have seen a ghost. This same woman also recounted stories she heard back then of people seeing Grace Sherwood standing in the fields near the house, waving to people as they passed by. Her spirit is said to haunt the houses that were later built in those fields.

During the legal battle surrounding what to do with Ferry Plantation House in the 1980s and early 1990s, the house sat empty for more than a decade. During this time, teenagers would often dare one another to go to the "haunted witch's house." Alpheus Chewning told one story where some teens went to explore the house one night. As they were approaching the front door, one of the guys fell through some rotten boards on the porch. A girl went on ahead and entered the house. Immediately, a huge owl flew out of the chimney into the room, and she ran screaming out of the house, convinced that the witch had flown out of the fireplace right at her. She ran all the way home, leaving her friend stuck on the porch.

It was during this time that ghost stories developed and grew as rumors of strange sights and sounds were reportedly coming from the abandoned house. Residents living on the Lynnhaven River who had docks facing the house claimed to see strange lights on the water, and sometimes in the mornings, they would find their lawn furniture turned to face the house. Jo Howren's ex-husband used to own Ferry Plantation, and she claims to have seen a young woman with dark hair walking from the dining room and through a pantry door. She was sure it was Grace Sherwood. Jo Howren

Grace Sherwood, Witch of Pungo. A second rendition by William George "Rip" Rylance. *Courtesy of the Friends of Ferry Plantation House.*

would go on to organize the Friends of Ferry Plantation House in 1996. Others claim that Grace's spirit appears with her dog or that she manifests as a ball of light around the house.

I have had guests and mediums alike tell me that while Grace isn't at Ferry all the time, she does make an occasional appearance. Those who knew Belinda say that she always believed that she was Grace reincarnated. This was given some credence one time when we were in the house with a medium. Her friend was using an ovilus, a paranormal app where words will appear either on their own or in response to questions. I asked the medium if Belinda's spirit was there in the house, and immediately, the name Grace appeared on the app. Gerry also tells of several times when they were hosting outdoor events at Ferry, and the weather forecast predicted rain. Belinda would tell her not to worry, that she would talk to Grace, and it would always end up being a beautiful day.

One of the claims for recognizing Belinda's spirit at Ferry Plantation is through the smell of her perfume. I personally have never experienced this at the house. However, one day, I decided to visit Grace's statue. It sits in the middle of a grassy area, surrounded by a parking lot and roads. There are no flowers or shrubs nearby. As I walked up to the statue that day, I got the strongest whiff of perfume. I looked around, and the only other person I saw was hundreds of feet away across the street, but there was no denying that I smelled perfume. I smiled and sat down on the bench in front of Grace's statue, feeling as if Belinda had come to visit Grace that day as well.

Grace Sherwood is a prominent figure in Virginia Beach history and folklore. Her life remains a mystery due to the lack of information and surviving records from her time. Centuries of creative imaginations have embellished her story to the point where it is now nearly impossible to separate fact from fiction. We are proud to continue to share her narrative at Ferry Plantation, as her legend has become an integral part of our history.

Acknowledgements

I would first like to thank the volunteers of Ferry Plantation who work countless hours to preserve and maintain this wonderful historic home. Their passion is contagious. Without their commitment to sharing Ferry, I would have never heard about the house, would never have volunteered, and it would never have become my second home. Gerry Richter and Ann Henley welcomed me in from the very beginning and taught me about the colonial lifestyle and traditions. They have served as role models for me in sharing the house with guests and in every other aspect of caring for a historic home. They both hold a special place in my heart. Cody Green has taught me nearly everything I know about the paranormal from investigating to the various equipment, and he can identify which spirits are in the house at any given time. His sense of humor and wonderful storytelling captured my attention on my very first visit. We continue to tackle the paranormal together, and I couldn't ask for a better mentor and friend. Joshua Husak keeps us straight on all things technological and social media related. As our resident skeptic, his level of suspicion makes for a great story when the unexplained happens. He does a great job keeping us online and in line as it relates to the technical running of the house. Cathy Hunt dedicates many hours to our gift shop, keeping our displays current and always finding new items to promote. Her love for the house is apparent, and I'll be forever grateful for her help in putting together my first colonial outfit. Cindy Core has become an invaluable member of Ferry with her enthusiasm for tours, events or in planning something new. She has great intuitive insight into the energy in the house. She is a hard worker, and I wouldn't want to be at

Ferry without her. Donovan Lenaghan is our fearless leader and voice of reason from many years of experience with the house. I feel Ruthe is my long-lost sister since we immediately bonded over the rather obscure history of the early Ferry Plantation families. She continues to be my paranormal overnight buddy, and I always learn something new when I'm with her. Most importantly, I'll always be beyond grateful for the true and enduring friendships I have made at Ferry. And I genuinely appreciate the trust and faith they put in me to tell Ferry's story before the first page of this book was ever written.

And I would also like to thank Belinda Nash, without whom we would only be able to refer to Ferry Plantation in the past tense. I never met Belinda, but her dedication and passion for the house is evident in every room. I have studied her abundant and thorough research on the history of the home, the land, its families and Grace Sherwood. She laid the groundwork for every aspect of this book from the history to the hauntings. While she passed away in 2016, her presence is still very much felt at Ferry.

I would like to give a huge thanks to my family for their continual encouragement on this project. My parents, Bill and Sue Mitchell, have always fully supported me in all of my endeavors. Growing up in a re-created colonial home designed by my mother and built mostly by my father, I couldn't help but learn to love history, as it surrounded me every day. My brother, Scott, modeled how to make the past come alive by serving as a tour guide at a local historic site. He also keeps me up to date on all of our own family history and stories. His wife, Roxy, is often my partner in crime as we attend numerous paranormal events. And thanks to my children, Bailey and Claudia, for always listening to my stories when I call and say, "Guess what happened at Ferry today?"

I would have been lost in a world of unclear concepts, mangled sentences, misspelled words and grammatical errors if it weren't for my editing gurus, Wendy Chamberlin and Kelly Parker. I cannot thank them enough for the hours they spent repairing my words and my stories through great insight and patience. They were also my cheerleaders throughout this entire process and gave me the strength and energy to keep pushing through.

I'd like to give a special shout-out to Scott Moore, who has become a trusted friend in the world of historical research and publishing. I greatly appreciate all the insight on Grace Sherwood and early Princess Anne County history. He also patiently answered my many questions as I learned to navigate the world of publishing. I'm thankful for all the support, even from the time when this book was just a thought.

I'm grateful for Al Chewning, who has inspired me with his local ghost stories and passion for Virginia Beach history. He serves as a great example of how to share history with hauntings and hauntings with history. He is an amazing author whose books influenced me to write this one. I appreciate his wonderful storytelling and for including me in local historical events.

I'd like to thank Peyton Townsend for sharing his stories from Ferry. It was great to get his insight from being involved with the house from a very young age.

I'm very appreciative of the patience and guidance from my acquisition editors, Laurie Krill and Kate Jenkins, at The History Press. They were fantastic to work with as they patiently guided me through this writing and publishing process.

A big thanks to Melissa Glover for the hours she spent with me at a local park, traipsing through wet grass to take my author photo. She is a talented photographer and a wonderful friend.

I want to thank my lifelong friend Amy Curtis, who is always ready for an adventure, especially if it is ghost related. We have spent many nights driving home at 3:00 a.m. from paranormal events, and I'll be forever grateful for her giving me my favorite ghost hunting T-shirt, which reads, "It's standing right behind me, isn't it?"

And a shout-out to my good friends David and Laarni Campbell for always being brave enough to ask, "How's the book coming along?" I wouldn't want to do life without their friendship. And thanks to their son, Brandon, who not only spent a summer scanning Ferry documents for me but also often came with me on Saturdays so I could open the house for tours.

Thank you to all the many others who have supported and encouraged me along this journey!

To everyone else who has dedicated time, energy and resources to protect and restore a historic location, thank you! It is often an uphill battle, but any time that a part of history is saved, we are able to continue the narrative so that people and places from the past can continue to have their stories told.

BIBLIOGRAPHY

American Syren and "Shipping" Illustrated. "Our Shipping Headlight: Charles M. Barnett, Esq." Vol. 5, no. 60 (December 19, 1903).

Anderson, Patricia Keppel. "12 Haunted Sites in Virginia with True Ghost Stories." Virginia Is for Lovers. https://www.virginia.org.

Archer, Michelle. "Fight Continues to Save Beach Home." *Virginian-Pilot*, April 1, 2003.

Attebery, Jennifer Eastman. *As Legend Has It: History, Heritage, and the Construction of Swedish American Identity*. University of Wisconsin Press, 2023.

Bahls, Roy A. "Things Go Bump in the Night at Eerie House." *Daily Break*, supplement of the *Virginian-Pilot*, October 30, 2005.

Baier, Sherry, 7 Cities Paranormal. Paranormal investigation notes from Ferry Plantation House, August 3, 2013.

Barrow, Mary Reid. "Architects Build Success into Ferry Plantation Renovation Efforts." *Virginia Beach Beacon*, November 28, 1999.

———. "Architects Examine Ferry Plantation for Restoration." *Virginian-Pilot*, February 14, 1998.

———. "An Historic Revival After Years of Neglect, the Ferry Plantation House Will Be Renovated, Preserving 300 Years of Local History." *Virginian-Pilot*, July 26, 1996.

Botham, Karen. "Ferry Plantation House Is Undergoing Preservation." *Virginia Beach Beacon*, March 4, 2001.

———. "Groups Tries Again for Ferry Farm Preservation Grant." *Virginia Beach Beacon*, February 14, 2002.

Bowers, Irene. "At 101, She's Still Celebrating Halloween Birthday." *Virginian-Pilot*, November 14, 2013.

———. "Remembering Belinda Nash." *Bayside Beacon* and *Virginian-Pilot*, May 17, 2016.

Brown, Catherine (Bunny). "Step Into the Past." *Ferry Tidings Newsletter* 7, no. 3 (July 2002).

Castleberry, Amy Hayes. *Virginia Beach (Then and Now)*. Arcadia Publishing, 2010.

Chewning, Alpheus J. *Haunted Virginia Beach*. The History Press, 2006.

Chubb, Tanaaz. "Finding Your Soul Place." Forever Conscious. https://foreverconscious.com.

Colonial Ghosts. "Top 25 Most Haunted Places in Virginia." https://colonialghosts.com.

Crist, Helen. "Old Fairfield House to Be Demolished." *Virginia Beach Sun*, February 17, 1972.

Daily Dispatch (Richmond, VA). May 21, 1862.

Daily Picayune 26, no. 94 (May 15, 1862).

Davis, Marc. "18th Century Artifacts Found at Ferry Farm." *Virginian-Pilot*, July 9, 1987.

Day, Joey. Personal interview with Belinda Nash, 2013.

Dickey, Colin. *Ghostland: An American History in Haunted Places*. Viking Press, 2016.

Discover Virginia Beach. "The Mansion, the Myth, and the Memories: Secrets of the Ferry Estate." Podcast, January 11, 2024. Available on YouTube. https://www.youtube.com.

Dufour, Charles L. *The Night the War Was Lost*. University of Nebraska Press, 1990.

Dunphy, Janet. "Ferry Plantation House Restoration Finds Surprises." *Virginia Beach Beacon*, April 22, 2004.

Elder, Angela Esco. *Love & Duty: Confederate Widows and the Emotional Politics of Loss*. University of Chapel Hill Press, 2022.

Fairlamb Sadler & Whitehead Architects, P.C. and Burkhart/Thomas Architecture—Interior Design. "A Study of the Ferry Plantation House." December 16, 1996.

"Featured Letter: A Wager Settled." Reprinted from *The Papers of Thomas Jefferson: Retirement Series.* Monticello Archives, Charlottesville, Virginia. www.monticello.org/sites/de812fault/files/inline-pdfs/TWilliamson19Dec1812.pdf.

Ferry Tidings Newsletter. "She Came Rolling Home." Vol. 17, no. 3 (October 2012).

———. "Step Into the Past, Part 32." Vol. 14, no. 4 (October 2009).

———. "What's in a Name?" Vol. 18, no. 1 (February 2013).

———. "Women of the Civil War." Vol. 14, no. 2 (April 2009).

Ford, Emily. "The Last Moments of Girod Street Cemetery." Oak & Laurel Cemetery Preservation. https://www.oakandlaurel.com.

Ford, Marlene. "Civic League Mulls Ferry Farm Ghost." *Virginian-Pilot*, September 23, 1999.

Founders Online, National Archives. "George McIntosh to Thomas Jefferson, 4 March 1812." https://founders.archives.gov. The original source is *The Papers of Thomas Jefferson, Retirement Series*, vol. 4, June 18, 1811, to April 30, 1812. Edited by J. Jefferson Looney. Princeton University Press, 2007.

———. "Thomas Jefferson to George McIntosh, 15 March 1812." https://founders.archives.gov. The original source is *The Papers of Thomas Jefferson, Retirement Series*, vol. 4, June 18, 1811, to April 30, 1812, edited by J. Jefferson Looney. Princeton University Press, 2007.

Franklin, Jennifer. "Haunted History Is Alive and Well in Virginia Beach." *USA Today*. https://www.usatoday.com.

Full Moon Paranormal Virginia. "The Ferry Plantation: Nanny EVP." June 6, 2015. Available on YouTube. https://www.youtube.com.

Gilbert, Lillie, Belinda Nash and Deni Norred-Williams. *Bayside History Trail: A View from the Water.* Eco Images, 2003.

———. *Ghosts, Witches & Weird Tales of Virginia Beach*. Eco Images, 2004.

Goldfard, Greg. "Championing Historic Home, Woman Invoked Cather." *Virginia Beach Beacon*, March 29, 1995.

Harms, Daniel. *Witch Bottles: History, Culture, Magic*. Avalonia, 2022.

Harris, Brenda. "At Home: Old Donation Farm, Virginia Beach Where Past and Present Nicely Blend." *Virginian-Pilot*, May 13, 1995.

Hellstrom, Carl. Personal interview with Belinda Nash, 2013.

History Goes Bump. "Ferry Plantation House and the Virginia Witch." Podcast. Episode 279, October 18, 2018.

Hudson, Carson O., Jr. *Witchcraft in Colonial Virginia*. The History Press, 2019.

Jaffé, Margaret Davis. "Princess Anne County Rich in Colonial Remains." *Virginian-Pilot*, February 28, 1926.

Jones, Matthew. "Historic Virginia Beach Home Up for Sale, Prompting Worry." *Virginian-Pilot* and *Chicago Tribune*, June 16, 2002.

Kellam, Sadie Scott, and V. Hope Kellam. *Old Houses in Princess Anne Virginia*. Printcraft Press Inc., 1958.

Keys, Jane Griffin. "The McIntosh Family of Scotland and Norfolk, Virginia." *Baltimore Sun*, February 9, 1908.

Kyle, Louisa Venable. *The History of Eastern Shore Chapel and Lynnhaven Parish, 1642–1969*. Teagle & Little Inc., 1969.

———. *The Witch of Pungo and Other Historical Stories of the Early Colonies*. Four O'Clock Farms Publishing Company, 1973.

Loyall, Camila Francis. *The Diary of Camilla Francis Loyall*. May 1, 1862–June 13, 1862. From Old Dominion University Library, Whittle Family Papers Collection. Norfolk, Virginia.

Mansfield, Stephen S. *Princess Anne County and Virginia Beach: A Pictorial History*. Donning Company, 1989.

McIntosh, Brenna. "Haunted Hampton Roads: The Ferry Plantation House in Virginia Beach." 13 News Now, October 21, 2022. https://www.13newsnow.com.

Moore, Scott O. *The Witch of Pungo: Grace Sherwood in Virginia History and Legend*. University of Virginia, 2024.

———. "The Witch of Pungo: The History Behind the Legend." Virginia Beach History Museums, Virginia Beach, Virginia, October 13, 2022.

Moss, Jeremy R. *Colonial Virginia's War Against Piracy: The Governor & the Buccaneer*. The History Press, 2022.

Mysteries at the Museum. "The Birth of the Road Map." Season 7, episode 5. Travel Channel. Episode features Belinda Nash. Aired May 1, 2015.

Nash, Belinda, and Danielle Sheets. *A Place in Time: The Age of the Witch of Pungo*. W.S. Dawson Company, 2012.

National Cyclopedia of American Biography. Published by James T. White and Company, circa 1928. http://lccn.loc.gov/2005681973.

Neleski, Patricia. "Ferry Plantation Researchers Plan 1830s Garden." *Virginia Beach Beacon*, April 15, 2005.

———. "Restoring Fireplace Found at Ferry Plantation House." *Virginian-Pilot*, March 14, 2006.

Norfolk Sun. "Colonial Days Again in Princess Anne." May 17, 1931.

Oddity Files. "Ferry Plantation." Season 1, episode 3. Directed by Kitsie Duncan, featuring Kitsie Duncan, Amanda Early and Chris Jay. Aired January 31, 2013.

Old Donation Episcopal Church. Virginia Beach, Virginia. https://1bob9.blogspot.com.

OmarGoshTV. "A Slave's Ghost Spoke to Me in This Haunted House." January 18, 2020. Available on YouTube. https://www.youtube.com.

Pennecke, Sandra Jill. "'Life on the Plantation' Offers Guest Perspectives." *Virginia Beach Beacon*, August 14, 2003.

Petretto, Cecilia. *Ghosts, Legends, and Lore of Hampton Roads*. Schiffer Publishing Ltd., 2010.

Reconnaissance Architectural Survey Report. City of Virginia Beach. Prepared by Frazier Associates, July 1992.

"Remote Sensing Investigations of Civil War Era Shipwrecks in the Vicinity of Fort. St. Philip, Plaquemines Parish, Louisiana." Appendix A: Letter from the Babcock Family Papers, 1862. U.S. Army Corps of Engineers, New Orleans District, April 1994.

Ricksecker, Mike. *Encounters with the Paranormal: Personal Tales of the Supernatural*. Vol. 4, *Ferry Plantation Edition*. Haunted Road Media, 2018.

Robbins, R. "Ferry Plantation, Haunted or Not? You Decide." May 5, 2015. Available on YouTube. https://www.youtube.com.

Rountree, Helen C. *The Powhatan Indians of Virginia: Their Traditional Culture*. University of Oklahoma Press, 1989.

Ruegsegger, Bob. "Ferry Plantation House Shows Its Holiday Spirit." *Virginia Beach Beacon*, November 10, 2011.

Sabella, Anthony. "Unfinished Business: An In-Depth Look at the Paranormal." New 3 WTKR, October 25, 2017. https://www.wtkr.com.

Salem (MA) Gazette 6, no. 90 (November 11, 1898). Walke Manor house fire announcement.

Star, Kris. "Little Ghost Girl Caught Singing on Video." January 22, 2020. Available on YouTube. https://www.youtube.com.

Statza, Gordon. Psychic medium's notes from visit to Ferry Plantation House, February 1997.

Stella Crowder Barnett obituary. *Virginian-Pilot* and *Norfolk Landmark*, October 13, 1912.

Sunday Delta 7, no. 24 (May 4, 1862). Louisiana, New Orleans.

Taylor, L.B., Jr. *The Ghosts of Tidewater…and Nearby Environs*. Progress Printing Company Inc., 1990.

———. *The Ghosts of Virginia*. Vol. 9. Progress Printing Company Inc., 2004.

Tazewell, Calvert. "Gleanings on Walk Family Homes." 1988. Archives 184, Box 1, Edgar T. Brown Collection, 1898–2007, Folder 3. Meyera E. Oberndorf Central Library, Virginia Beach, Virginia.

Travel and Leisure Magazine. "Best Haunted Places in Every State." https://www.travelandleisure.com.

Try to Scare Me. "Ferry Plantation House: Virginia Beach, VA." http://www.trytoscareme.

Turner, Florence Kimberly. *Gateway to the New World: A History of Princess Anne County, Virginia, 1607–1824*. Southern Historical Press Inc., 1984.

Vaughan, Trefor Doloughan. "Fact and Fiction in a Legend." *Folklore* 119, no. 2 (2008): 218–32.

Virginia: A Guide to the Old Dominion. Writers' Program of the Work Projects Administration. Oxford University Press, 1940.

Virginia Beach Public Library. *The Beach: A History of Virginia Beach, Virginia*. Department of Public Libraries, 2006.

Virginia Magazine of History and Biography. "Families of Lower Norfolk and Princess Anne Counties." Vol. 5, no. 2 (October 1897). Virginia Historical Society.

Virginia Military Institute Archives. "A Guide to the Thomas H. Williamson Papers, 1788, 1850–1888." Lexington, Virginia. https://archivesspace.vmi.edu.

Virginian-Pilot and *Norfolk Landmark*. "Toadstools the Cause of Death: Mrs. Stella Barnett Dies at Protestant Hospital from Effect of Poison." October 12, 1912.

Walke, Henry, Rear Admiral, USN. "Private Record of the Walke Family in the United States." *Brief Records and Recollections of the Walke Family and Relations in the United States*. 1887. Ferry Plantation House Archives.

Weintraub, Karen. "Neighbors Don't Want House to Be a Home, but a Family Hopes to Move into the Supposedly Haunted Ferry Farm House." *Virginian-Pilot*, September 14, 1994.

William and Mary Walke estate records, 1798–1804. Princess Anne County, Virginia. Ferry Plantation House Archives.

Worley, Connor. "Haunted Hampton Roads: The Ghosts of Virginia Beach's Ferry Plantation House." WHRO, October 17, 2023. https://www.whro.org.

Wyatt-Brown, Bertram. *Southern Honor: Ethics and Behavior in the Old South*. Oxford University Press Inc., 2007.

Yarsinske, Amy Waters. *Lost Virginia Beach*. The History Press, 2011.

Personal Interviews

Core, Cindy. Personal interview, February 10, 2024.

Green, Cody. Personal interview, January 6, 2024.

Henley, Ann. Personal interview, February 10, 2024.

Hunt, Cathy. Personal interview, February 10, 2024.

Husak, Joshua. Personal interview, February 6, 2024.

Lenaghan, Donovan. Personal interview, February 10, 2024.

Lenaghan, Lauren. Personal interview, July 5, 2024.

Lenaghan, Margaret. Personal Interview, February 10, 2024.

Richter, Gerry. Personal interviews, August 18, 2020; February 10, 2024; and June 29, 2024.

Ruthe. Personal interview, March 9, 2024.

Townsend, Peyton. Personal interview, December 9, 2024.

INDEX

About the Author

Photo by Melissa Glover.

Kristen Ellis has served as the director of historical research for the Friends of Ferry Plantation House (FOFPH) in Virginia Beach, Virginia, since 2020. She dedicates much of her free time to Ferry Plantation by giving tours, hosting special events and researching the history of the home. A graduate of the University of Virginia, Kristen comes from a family of historians and was raised to appreciate the importance of protecting and preserving historic sites. She has always been fascinated with the paranormal, and you can often find her visiting haunted locations or exploring old cemeteries. A former high school teacher with experience in traveling and living abroad, Kristen now works in the field of international education. *Haunted Ferry Plantation* is her first book.